JOURNEY'S END

THE TRUTH ABOUT LIFE AFTER DEATH

COLM KEANE

CAPEL
ISLAND

First published in Ireland in 2022

by

CAPEL ISLAND PRESS
Baile na nGall,
Ring, Dungarvan,
County Waterford,
Ireland

ISBN 978-0-9559133-8-9

Printed and bound by Clays Ltd, Elcograf S.p.A
Typesetting and cover design by Typeform Ltd

For Seán

Colm Keane has written 30 books, including eight number one bestsellers, among them *Going Home, We'll Meet Again* and *Heading for the Light.* He is a graduate of Trinity College, Dublin, and Georgetown University, Washington DC. As a broadcaster, he won a Jacob's Award and a Glaxo Fellowship for European Science Writers. His books, spanning 19 chart bestsellers, include *The Distant Shore* and *Forewarned.*

CONTENTS

Death is not extinguishing the light; it is only putting out the lamp because the dawn has come.

Rabindranath Tagore
Indian poet and Nobel Prize winner,
1861 – 1941

INTRODUCTION

You will struggle to find a more conclusive portrayal of what we face after death than in the pages of this book. What you will read draws together many years of inquiry into a vast array of sources, including near-death experiences, vision reports, ancient religious texts and the latest studies from the world of science. They establish, with remarkable clarity, the otherworld we move to after we die.

You will see in the chapters ahead how death is not an end but the start of something totally new. You will discover how our consciousness survives in a heaven or hell of our own making. An afterlife of peace and tranquillity will be revealed. Why we meet with deceased relatives and friends, including children and pets, will be explained. Above all, you will learn the need for preparation if you wish to ensure a happy death.

Since 2009, I have written several books about the journey we make once our heart stops beating and our brain flat-lines. These books – *Going Home*, *The Distant Shore*, *We'll Meet Again* and *Heading for the Light* – have deliberately stopped short of describing what happens in the hereafter, concentrating instead on our journey to the edge of death. A new sphere of investigation, however, has expanded our knowledge of the subject.

New evidence has emerged from an area of physics known as quantum mechanics (QM). Not only has it blown apart our understanding of the universe, but it has also provided a sound basis for believing that our consciousness lives on in the hereafter.

Quantum investigations have also made sense of the existing evidence supporting the concept of post-death survival.

With quantum mechanics as a backdrop, descriptions of the afterlife from those who have near-death experiences suddenly make sense. Claims about post-death survival stretching from the early Egyptians through numerous other cultures, including Greece and Rome, can be assessed afresh. The great spiritual texts underpinning Christianity, Buddhism, Hinduism and Islam can be understood in a new light. Even the images described by mystics and visionaries seem to fall into place. You will see why this is so by the end of this book.

I cannot adequately describe my reactions when I first delved into the quantum sphere. It was like scales falling away from my eyes. The minor – yet niggling – differences in the experiences of people who undergo temporary death were no longer a cause for concern. The central messages of the Bible, the Koran, the great texts of Hinduism and Buddhism, gelled together in a thrilling explanation of after-death survival. The inner sense most of us share that life doesn't end with death was validated and shown to be justified.

Inconsistencies between world religions suddenly no longer mattered. They all reflected the same fundamental journey – survival after death, travel to the light, the existence of some sort of 'supreme being', and other features including meetings with deceased relatives and friends. Most of all, they were all exponents of the primacy of light. This book brings you as close as you will get to an understanding of that light.

There will be many twists and turns along the way. You will read how various world faiths, with their harrowing imagery and inflamed rhetoric, their rules and regulations, have distorted the truth about what happens after death. You will see how depictions of hell and the devil, along with domains such as purgatory and Limbo, have little or no bearing on what you face after you die.

Along the way I will familiarise you with the development not only of religious thinking but of *all* thinking, scientific and otherwise, in our search for the truth about the afterlife. The works of St. Augustine, St. Thomas Aquinas, Pope St. Gregory I, the Venerable Bede, Bernard of Cluny, Mechthild of Magdeburg, among many others, will be examined and drawn from.

So, too, will the Egyptian Book of the Dead, Tibetan Book of the Dead, Bhagavad Gita, the Vedas and Puranas of Hinduism and, of course, the Koran, the Torah and the books of the Old and New Testaments. I will help you thread your way through these texts, separating fact from fiction, and extracting from them their ultimate truths.

I hope you will find this book an easy and interesting read. That is what I have attempted to achieve. At each stage, the writing is kept as simple as possible, and even the science is explained in an everyday way. Bear with me and, by the end, I guarantee that you will have a greater understanding than you have ever had about what happens when we reach the other side.

Colm Keane

THE REALM OF LIGHT

At first there was a brilliant, bright light. It was clearly visible in the distance. Eileen was travelling towards it, accompanied by three 'beings of light'. She desperately wanted to reach it. It was the ultimate destination, the journey's end, the place where she wanted to be. She knew she was going there and would soon be in paradise, in the company of God.

At the time, Eileen was undergoing emergency surgery having haemorrhaged internally following an ectopic pregnancy. 'I was completely gone and so near dying,' she later explained. She had been rushed to hospital by ambulance, wheeled at speed down a corridor, staff undressing her as they went. The surgical team set to work, suturing and removing the embryo.

The patient, however, was no longer there. Instead, Eileen had left her body and was heading towards a distant bright radiance that she knew to be heaven and the home of God. She was floating upwards with the three 'beings of light' holding her in their arms. 'They weren't people, but they were so beautiful,' she recalled. 'They were made of light, and so full of peace and joy. I was very happy.'

Although it was daytime, the sky's blackness contrasted with the sheer brightness ahead. 'It was a big, big light in the sky,' Eileen said. 'It was as if a lot of electric lights were lighting up the whole place. The light was really beautiful and it wasn't hurting my eyes. There was a wonderful sense of peace. The feeling of love was amazing. I was wrapped in it and I was very,

very happy. I know it was heaven ahead. I know it was God up there. It was so beautiful that I used to cry afterwards hoping to get back there.'

Having travelled close to the light, Eileen suddenly stopped short. 'I had the sensation of falling,' she recollected. 'I went flying downwards and I was back into my bed in the hospital. I opened my eyes. The surgeon was there and he said, "Welcome back!" He later told me that I was a miracle. I will never forget what he said to me. He said, "You bought your ticket, but you didn't travel!"'

The single most important feature that sums up heaven is the presence of light. People who die temporarily – perhaps for five minutes or so before returning to their bodies – commonly remark on it. It is often the first thing they observe – a bright luminescence, a star-like or sun-like radiance, normally at a distance, drawing them to it. It is usually seen at the end of the tunnel through which they are travelling.

They desperately want to get to it, knowing it is the pinnacle of love, peace and happiness, the home of the superior being or God. Some find themselves instantly in the light. Others approach it gradually. Nothing else matters only to enter it. Even those who have good reasons not to die suddenly want to do so. All are overwhelmed by the profound sense of joy, wonder and warmth they experience at the prospect of being in the light.

Most world religions have heavenly light at their core. Prophets and messiahs have been inspired by it. Sacred texts are filled with references to it. Hymns, poems, psalms, songs of praise have been composed to celebrate it. Well-known faiths have even fought battles and wars over it, with each aspiring to become 'the religion of light'.

6

An intense feeling of love is experienced either in the light or on the way to the light. It is difficult to explain what it is like. It is certainly not like the love of physical attraction. Nor does it involve the love of material things. Instead, it is a selfless outpouring of tenderness and affection towards others and towards the source of all love – the superior being, or God.

People struggle to describe how profound and intense this love can be. They use words like euphoric, ecstatic or overpowering. One woman spoke of feeling 'wrapped up' in it. A man found it so comforting, so joyous, so satisfying that he wanted to lose himself forever in the wonder of it. Most say it is unlike any experience you could ever imagine.

Anne described well the feeling of love in the light. 'I was bathed in a beautiful, greenish-yellow light, almost fluorescent but not severe,' she told me. 'It was like no other colour I had ever seen before. It was healing and soothing, like a loving light. It's hard to explain, but there was healing and love in one feeling. It was the most beautiful, peaceful feeling I ever experienced in my entire life. It was like I was in a resting place.

'There was a great feeling of love there, like you were being wrapped up in it. It wasn't a physical love; it was more spiritual. It wasn't like the feeling I had after giving birth. I thought I had known everything about love after holding my child for the first time. But this was different; it was euphoric and ecstatic. I've never experienced that kind of love here on earth.'

Heavenly experiences like these are by no means associated with the religiously inclined or with God-fearing fanatics. Studies, if anything, show that religious affiliation has no bearing in determining what happens. Instead, the experience is common to everyone irrespective of age, sex, race or creed.

Christians have these joyful experiences. So, also, do Hindus, Buddhists, Muslims and many more. Even atheists, who believe there is no God, or agnostics, who believe that God is unknown and unknowable, experience them, too. In the vast majority of these cases, the feeling of peace in the light is nothing short of profound.

'There was the greatest sensation of peace I have ever felt,' Bernard, a car crash survivor, told me. 'It wasn't of this world. Everything was totally quiet and I felt completely relaxed. There was no fear of any kind. It's impossible to put proper words on it, it was so joyful. You certainly wouldn't experience it on this earth.

'I honestly felt it was the sort of peace you would only get from being in the presence of God. I think I was very close to him. It's probably the big reason why if I were to die today or tomorrow I wouldn't be afraid. It was complete peace and I hope I get to experience it again one day.'

It is common for people to experience together some or all of the heavenly elements mentioned so far – the light, love, peace and sensing the presence of a 'superior being' or God. Each element blends into the other, enhancing what is happening and elevating it to a level of supreme joy. The total effect is greater than the sum of its parts. Multiplied in that way, the impact is overwhelming.

This mixture of elements has been reported by many of my interviewees, including Eddie, who undertook a journey following an attempted suicide. A dazzling incandescence dominated his recollections. The strength and radiance of the glow that encompassed him, he commented, was beyond words. The light was

accompanied by peaceful, loving feelings unparalleled by anything known on earth. There was also a sense of timelessness.

'I cannot describe the light, it was so unbelievable,' Eddie
explained. 'It was a different kind of light than what we talk
about here. This light was so beautiful and peaceful. I was at
perfect peace and had no knowledge of past or future. I had
nothing on my mind. I was just there. If there's such a thing as
"perfect peace", that was it. It must have been the peace of
heaven. I say that because of the impact the light had on me
and the effect it had on me. It is hard to describe.'

Light, with its power to bring warmth, growth and peace to
mankind, has formed the backbone of man's otherworld beliefs
since the beginning of time. Our earliest forebears knew of its
importance. They comprehended that without light we wouldn't
exist. As far back as 14 or so centuries before Christ, they spoke
about it with reverence and awe.

'Let there be light!' declared the Book of Genesis, reputedly
written by Moses around the 1300s BC. Describing the origins
of the universe, he immediately identified light. It was, he said,
the light that separated us from the darkness. The light brought
us our day; the darkness our night. 'God saw that the light was
good,' he declared, and only after he created it did we have life.

How remarkably insightful those first lines of Genesis proved
to be. As we now know from science, Moses was right. Billions
of years ago, when our world sprang into life, bringing us the
galaxies and stars, it was all down to light. From a soup-like
mush of energy came light. Without it, there would have been
no creation, no mankind and no life.

Somehow our earliest ancestors understood this primacy of
light. No better example of the importance attributed to it can
be found than at Newgrange in Ireland – a place name that

translates from the Gaelic as 'The Cave of the Sun'. It was here that early man constructed an extraordinary structure 5,200 years ago, many centuries before the Egyptian pyramids or Stonehenge, and some 3,000 years before Christ.

At the winter solstice, the light of the sun travels down the passage entrance of the structure, penetrating the earth at a time when darkness is at its greatest. The sequence of events is extraordinary. Slowly the sun rises over a nearby mountain, bathing Newgrange in light. With eerie precision, a light shaft penetrates the monument's passageway, gradually working its way until it illuminates the deep interior, before retreating and returning the monument to relative darkness.

What we observe at Newgrange is uncannily reflected in the stories of people who have near-death experiences. 'I found myself in this tunnel,' said Ann. 'The tunnel was like a dark void. It surrounded me. If I was to describe it, it would have been about six feet wide and about the same height. The walls were just darkness. I was passing through it, walking. I was moving quite freely, at a comfortable pace.

'At the end of the tunnel was this light. It was about 50 yards away. It wasn't a sharp light, just shimmering and appealing. It was more yellow in colour, like sunshine. It was like a space that was lit by the sun. It was a little bit like if you were walking in a forest and you saw a glade, you'd want to go to it. It's like an instinctive thing – you'd want to come out of the darkness. I just wanted to go to the light.'

The light continued to feature in civilisations that followed Newgrange. It was at the heart of ancient Egyptian beliefs, where the most powerful deity was the sun god Ra. As far back as 2,500 years before Christ, he was seen to traverse the sky, rising in the east each day, bringing light to the world, before dying in the west after leaving the moon in place to brighten up the sky. By night, he was said to travel through the underworld, providing illumination for the souls of the dead.

Sun and light were integral to the reign of this powerful solar god. He journeyed across the sky in a sun boat, spitting out the stars each night and creating humans from his tears. His temples were opened up to the sunlight and contained neither statues nor icons. It is even said that the shape of the Egyptian pyramids, radiating upwards to a peak, may represent the rays of the sun associated with this potent and popular deity.

By the time of Christ, many religions shared this obsession with the dazzling brilliance of light. It was everywhere – in their doctrines and teachings, in their dogmas and beliefs. It might be said that the rivalry between them represented a contest for the supreme accolade of 'religion of the light'.

What they clearly understood by 'light' was a lot more than the illumination provided by the sun or any other incandescence which might help us to see. Instead, they had in mind the 'light' pertaining to our capacity for perception and comprehension, and in particular for grasping the meaning of life and the world around us.

They understood that just as light had powered creation, so too did this extraordinary ability of God's creatures – this ability to perceive and comprehend – power the essence of what we are. Both forms of light are fundamental to the universe. They are timeless and without any mass. Above all, they are very close companions in explaining the greater reality of the meaning and purpose of life.

'The light is wisdom and love beyond all comprehension,' said one woman, Dr. Dianne Morrissey, following her near-death experience. 'Within the light of God, we realise that everyone and everything is connected to God. In the light is the cure for all diseases, the knowledge within every universe.'

Anni, who also underwent a near-death experience, perceived a similar universal truth. 'I had this awareness of an enormous consciousness of which mine was a part,' she remarked. 'My consciousness was released from its bodily form. The bodily form was completely insignificant. It was like a drop in the ocean and part of something much, much bigger. I had this distinct sense that it could reach anywhere. There was this feeling of reaching across space.'

This perception of a greater global consciousness was likewise experienced by Paula, who travelled to the light during a serious illness in 1985. 'The light was like it was pouring through and coming from something way beyond which was much bigger,' Paula recalled. 'I knew that when I got to it there would be this being of absolute goodness. Everything to do with good, like creativity and kindness, would be there. I don't know how I knew that, but I did.

'All of that was coming up in the light. The light was calling me along. It was crystal white. It was very shiny, as if reflecting on itself. The whole end of the tunnel was painted with this light. I wasn't going anywhere else but there.'

The world's first organised religions were quickly off the mark, presenting us with light-filled images of life after death. It began with the Persian prophet Zoroaster, who lived a long time ago, probably around 600 years before Christ. The religion he inspired was preoccupied with light. Another religion active at the time sprung from devotion to the Persian divinity Mithra. It, too, propagated the message of light.

Many of Mithraism's light motifs, including those linked to Zoroastrianism, were incorporated in the next big follow-on religion – Christianity. Anyone scrutinising the Christian New Testament might legitimately believe that the work is some sort of manifesto of light, written for the 'children of light,' as followers are described. For those who believe in God, they 'shall not walk in darkness, but shall have the light of life.' For them, at life's end, heaven beckons and the goal is clear – eternal life in the light.

Although Christianity's doctrine was powerful and appealing, it was at the time lagging behind yet another religious creed, Manichaeism – named after the Persian prophet Mani – which also had light at its core. Manichaean theology was underpinned by the belief that there are two conflicting realms – the realm of light and the realm of darkness.

The religion's 'elect' eat vegetarian foods, primarily because they are believed to be full of light. Its main deity lives in the Paradise of Light, where gods and angels reside in a halo of luminescence. The souls of those who ascend to an afterlife pass on to the Paradise of Light.

While these light-based religions were battling each other over 2,000 years ago, many near-death experiences and out-of-body experiences, with their numerous references to heavenly light, were being recorded and documented. Even in the New Testament, there was at least one fascinating real-life story – involving St. Paul.

St. Paul, who authored a large portion of the New Testament – Romans, Galatians, Ephesians, Philippians and many more books and letters – described having once been 'caught up into paradise,' adding 'whether I was in my body or out of my body,

I don't know,' using a phrase readily identifiable to those who have had a near-death experience. His comments most likely referred to his conversion on the road to Damascus, which he described elsewhere in the New Testament.

Writing about the dramatic occurrence, he outlined how while travelling along he was enveloped by light. 'Suddenly a light from heaven' flashed around him, was how he described the startling event. Not surprisingly, St. Paul went on to espouse the importance of love in his writings, as so many near-death survivors do. He also wrote that he had no fear of death – 'Where, o death, is your victory? Where, o death, is your sting?' – reflecting the sort of calm that near-death survivors feel about dying.

It was around the same time period that other narratives relating to the concept of a soul departing from the body and travelling to heavenly light were put down in black and white. They appeared in *The Republic* by Plato and *On the Delays of the Divine Vengeance* by Plutarch. The first work was written around four centuries before Christ, the second within a century of his death.

I have alluded to Plato's story of Er time and again, primarily because of its landmark significance in identifying man's early understanding of the death process. This was no recounting of pagan myth or religious belief; instead, it was a clear articulation of a phenomenon we have only now come to scientifically explore but which was recognised four centuries before the birth of Christ.

The warrior Er, we are told, was killed in battle. Ten days after being slain, his body was found unaffected by decay and was carried home for burial. On the twelfth day, while lying on his funeral pyre, he returned to life and told a remarkable tale.

He described how, when he was slain, 'his soul left the body' and 'went on a journey.' Arriving in a 'mysterious place,' he witnessed the judging of souls and, most importantly, encountered the light. He described 'a line of light, straight as a column, extending right through the whole heaven and through the earth, in colour resembling the rainbow, only brighter and purer.'

The light, he said, was 'the belt of heaven, and holds together the circle of the universe.' He used another allusion to light when describing how souls moved on to their new lives – they were 'like stars shooting,' he said. After encountering identifiable souls, he then returned to his body. On waking, he 'found himself lying on the pyre.'

The second reference to light in the afterlife came from the Greek historian and essayist Plutarch, who lived in the latter half of the first century into the beginning of the second century. He chronicled the story of a man named Thespesius who died having fallen from a height on to his neck. 'The fall beat the breath out of his body,' was how Plutarch described his passing.

Three days later, as they were about to bury him, he came back to life. Not only had his 'sense' left his body at the time of the fall, he said, but he 'saw stars of a vast magnitude, at an immense distance one from the other, and sending forth a light most wonderful for the brightness of its colour.'

He recalled many features of the otherworld, including its inhabitants. Some of the souls he encountered, he said, 'shone like a round body of perfect light, and were transparent within.' Others exuded 'a smooth, even, and contiguous lustre.' One of the souls recognised him and took him on a journey through the various regions of the afterlife where, once again, light played a prominent role.

He described how, at one stage, he travelled so quickly yet so gently that he seemed to be 'borne upon the rays of the light as upon wings.' He also remarked at another point how 'the extraordinary brightness of the light dazzled his eyes.' All this came to an end when he was forced through a pipe (a reference very familiar today) and awoke to find himself 'on the brink of his own grave.'

Time and again, right up to the present day, one report after the other has replicated these earliest-known experiences of after-death survival and heavenly bliss. Numerous accounts provided by people ranging from saints to the man in the street have described how the 'other self' – the soul, mind, spirit or consciousness – left their bodies and travelled on a peaceful, warm journey to a new life in the light.

A few examples are worth highlighting. Heaven, according to the seventh- and early eighth-century Irish saint, Adamnán, who had a near-death experience, was full of light and covered in a beautiful fragrance – a joyous, noble and splendid place where only happiness reigns. Another account, from around the same time, describes the experience of a French lawyer, magistrate and monk by the name of Salvius, who died only to return to life shortly afterwards.

Salvius described how, after dying, he travelled beyond the sun, moon and stars to the highest peak of heaven. He was eventually directed to a place of great wonder. 'Over this place there hung a cloud more brilliant than any light, and yet no sun or moon or star could be seen,' he said. 'Indeed, the cloud shone more brightly than any of these with its own brilliance.' There he was greeted by 'a number of beings,' some in ordinary dress, others dressed in priestly vestments. He soon heard a disembodied voice saying 'Let this man go back into the world,' after which he travelled back the way he had come, weeping as he departed.

A further report is worth mentioning briefly, this one dating from the eighteenth century. The account appeared in a French medical book, *Anecdotes de Médecine*, which was written by the physician Pierre-Jean du Monchaux. Recounting the story of one of his patients – a well-known Parisian pharmacist – Monchaux described how the man 'saw such a pure and extreme light that he thought he was in heaven.' He felt he was in the 'Kingdom of the Blessed.' He also reported a peaceful sensation and said that never in his life had he experienced a nicer moment.

Why we encounter this 'light of all lights' at the point of death is pivotal to understanding what happens when we die. For centuries, the question of why the body's slide into oblivion should end in bright luminescence and not just in total darkness has defied explanation. It has baffled neuroscientists. They have been unable to account for it. Even if they can attempt explanations for other aspects of the near-death experience, they cannot do the same for light.

Modern quantum mechanics, however, has provided us with new and stunning insights which I will examine towards the end of this book. These insights will reveal how we might indeed survive physical death and spend an afterlife basking in the light of a heaven or paradise. In the meantime, we need to delve deeper into our realm of light and focus on its principal occupant, often referred to as Yahweh, Jehovah, Allah, Brahma or, more often in the West, simply as God.

MEETING GOD

There is a memorable scene in the epic film *The Ten Commandments*, which was released in 1956. Having been drawn to a burning bush, Moses found himself in the presence of God. The scene must have seemed strange to cinema audiences unfamiliar with the Bible, especially when God's voice emerged from the bush. Moses, realising who it was, dropped to the ground.

Perhaps because film technology was relatively primitive in the 1950s, the flaming bush looked like a Christmas shop window decoration with an orange light glowing in the background. The casting for the fiery scene was even more peculiar, with a relatively young Charlton Heston – then in his early 30s – playing Moses, and the sonorous voice of God also being provided by Heston.

From a biblical point of view, the scene is important. This was the moment God informed Moses that he had selected him to lead his 'chosen people' out of Egypt. He also used the expression 'I am who I am' when asked by Moses to identify his name. Just as important, God revealed himself from the 'burning bush', thereby identifying the sense of brightness or light that would characterise him from that time to the present.

This epic interpretation of the story of Moses became one of the greatest financial successes in cinematic history. It was seen by millions of Christians at the time of its release and was later played for schoolchildren and on TV throughout the

Western world. Known for its huge scale, it emblazoned on people's minds the concept of a powerful and authoritative God – mysterious, disembodied and, above all, immersed in light.

The film was true to the Bible in that it didn't show the features of God. This idea of God's features being inscrutable is stressed in the Gospel of John, where it is stated that 'no one has seen God at any time.' The remark is consistent with other biblical references, notably in a further encounter between God and Moses where Moses is told: 'You cannot see my face; for no man shall see me and live.'

This indecipherability of God's features is uncannily replicated in the near-death experience. One man I interviewed, who had temporarily died during heart surgery, saw what he felt was a tall being dressed in a habit. He caught sight of this figure over his left shoulder. When he glanced at the face, however, he could see 'no face, only blackness.' The face was completely blacked out.

Another interviewee, who was involved in a near-drowning, reported that he could not discern any facial features, either, although he was close to the figure that appeared before him. 'I could see no face,' he told me. 'I thought that was quite extraordinary.' Interestingly, each time the idea of God would enter the man's head, the ambient light would become brighter and brighter, implying God's connection to light more than anything of a physical nature.

Similar comments have been made by near-death survivors from throughout the world. They adhere to a set pattern. An American described seeing a figure bathed in light which, while looking like a human, had no distinct facial features. Another person, from New Zealand, replicated the comment in the previous paragraph when he described how the light intensified every time he looked towards the face of a figure in front of him. He couldn't make out the face, either.

The conclusions drawn by a further person – an Oklahoma schoolteacher – were almost identical. The woman in question left her body in 2009 following an unexpected reaction to pain medication used during her treatment for pancreatitis. Apart from tunnel travel and bright lights, she also experienced God, but not physically.

'I didn't see the human form of God,' Crystal McVea recalled in an interview. 'I didn't see hands and feet and a face. I just saw the most beautiful light.' She could, however, see, smell, taste, touch and hear God but with more than the five senses she had on earth. She could also speak to God but without using words.

This impossibility of seeing – or describing – God's physical features, as expressed by many religions and outlined by those who experience near-death, has created innumerable problems for artists down through the ages. In a world where images are indispensible for imparting information, the inherent difficulties are readily apparent. These complications have stretched the imaginations of book illustrators, painters and graphic artists when portraying one of the most sought-after images in history.

Early Jewish and Christian artists came up with the idea of depicting the 'hand of God' instead of God's physical form. A hand normally extending to the wrist but sometimes including part of the arm would be drawn or painted. It typically appeared from a cloud or from the top border of the artwork. Examples are numerous and can be seen in one of the earliest-known synagogues – the third-century Dura-Europos, located in Syria – and in the fourth-century catacombs in Rome.

Other artistic representations featured images depicting the 'Ancient of Days'. The phrase derives from the Book of Daniel, where the Son of Man is said to have come to the 'Ancient of Days' and was presented with a 'dominion, and glory, and a kingdom' which 'shall not pass away' or 'be destroyed.' This text was written somewhere around two centuries before Christ.

The Ancient of Days describes a God who is not only old but timeless. 'He is both before eternity and above eternity and his kingdom, a kingdom of all the ages,' was how St. Dionysius put it. Translated into practical terms, an effusion of images followed which showed God as a bearded old man, venerable and wise, trustworthy and philosophical, thoughtful and fair-minded.

Perhaps the most obvious reason for the indecipherability of God's physical features is that they don't exist. In other words, he has no bodily form. Without a corporeal presence, there is nothing to describe. This may well explain why survivors of near-death experiences, along with most established religions, invariably refer to God as a light-enveloped, non-physical 'supreme being' or 'superior being' or 'being of light' full of goodness, warmth, love, peace, tenderness, compassion and understanding.

Given that this may be so, perhaps artists down through the ages were clever in opting for either symbolic representations of God as a hand or arm, or figurative representations of God's qualities as personified in a bearded old man. To do otherwise would have been to betray the reality of what God is. It was their way of expressing what, in truth, would appear to be an ephemeral, cosmic, universal God – a huge power beyond our comprehension that drives the universe and represents all that is good including light, love and life.

Without any doubt, the most common feature associated with God, either in accounts from those who have temporarily died or in ancient texts, is the bright, warm, comforting light that constitutes his essence. Almost everyone, on their return from death, remembers it vividly. They describe how God's light drew them to it, like pins to a magnet. They desperately wanted to reach it. It overwhelmed them, washed over them, changed their lives and left them longing to return to it one day.

'It's almost too difficult to describe in words,' Michelle , who haemorrhaged following a childbirth, remarked about God's light. 'I realise I was in the presence of God. When I consider the light, and the way I felt in the light – the glow and the warmth and the comfort and the peace and the happiness – they are all the things you would associate with the supreme, higher being and the place we will all go to after we die.

'The more I think about it and talk about it, the more I believe that's where I was – in the presence of God. But it's not something that can really be described. Maybe nobody can really understand unless they have been there. It's not just what you see there; it's the feeling you get of peace and beauty and love and all the things you would associate with God or heaven. It's really hard to describe.'

In the last chapter we read how those who die head towards a 'realm of light'. As they begin their journey, the light often appears as a simple speck in the distance. It gets brighter as they approach it. Those who die are curious but they aren't always sure why they need to get to it. Yet they still know it marks their final resting place or, as the title of this book calls it, their 'journey's end'.

At some stage on their journey, they come to recognise that this ultimate destination, this last port of call, 'the dominion of light', really is a lot more than that. Not only is God in the light or behind the light, but he might even *be* the light itself. Indeed, the light may be all the wisdom, goodness, kindness and truth, infinite and eternal, that we associate with God – in other words, God himself.

That this may be so has been remarked upon by many who have come into the light's presence. A case in point is Dr. Rajiv Parti, who was born in India and brought up as a Hindu, and who later worked as an anaesthesiologist in the USA. Diagnosed with prostate cancer in 2008, he developed a range of medical complications culminating in his admission to hospital with sepsis, a life-threatening infection.

Not only did he depart his body while undergoing treatment, but he entered a tunnel and travelled to God's light. He described it as a 'glowing white light', which was calming, loving, formless and bluish in colour. The light, he explained, was an entity which he 'knew' was 'supreme love, knowledge and intelligence personified.'

'It is hard to describe in words how it felt to be in the presence of the Light Being,' he reflected. 'Pure love pervaded everything, as if all the five earthly senses were soaked in love. It was present everywhere, and all-powerful. My consciousness felt merged with the supreme primordial consciousness. I was at once communicating with it and in it.'

Dr. Parti felt deep joy and inner peace. The Light Being told him he was experiencing cancer so that he might have empathy for the suffering of others. He was also informed that it wasn't his time and that his future lay in helping others with diseases of the soul, chronic pain, addiction and depression. This he did on his return to life.

Another person who encountered a great 'God of light' was George Ritchie, an American who died temporarily from a severe case of pneumonia in December 1943. Twenty years of age and an army recruit at the time, he had already completed premedical education at university and would later go on to become an eminent psychiatrist. On that winter's day, in 1943, he spiked a fever of 106.5 degrees Fahrenheit while being treated in hospital. He left his body and headed for God's light.

There was an incredible intensity and brightness to the 'man made out of light' he encountered. He immediately understood this being to be power itself, older than time, 'the Son of God'. 'All the light bulbs in the ward could not give off that much light,' Ritchie recalled. 'All the bulbs in the world could not! It was impossibly bright: it was like a million welders' lamps all blazing at once.'

Emanating from this being of light was enormous, unconditional love – 'a love beyond my wildest imagining,' he said. In its presence, he undertook a life review and was also given a guided tour through hell and a distant view of heaven, before eventually returning to his body a transformed man.

It is no surprise to discover that the idea of God being light is repeatedly referred to in scripture and in other sacred texts. Indeed, if there is one specific aspect of the near-death experience that is replicated with almost pinpoint accuracy in most ancient religious manuscripts it is the concept of divine light.

The light of God is nowhere more prominent than in the Bible. The Christian God lives in the light, *is* the light and is the source of all light. 'God is light, and in him is no darkness at all,' is how it is put. He is variously described in terms of his radiance – as 'a burning and a shining light' and a 'marvellous light.' His son, Jesus, has come as a 'light from heaven,' as 'the light of the world' or 'the light of men,' his purpose being to 'bear witness' to his father's light.

Even in the Old Testament, God's light is ever-present. The Lord, we learn from these ancient writings, 'wraps himself in light as with a garment.' We see references to the light on God's face. His 'everlasting light' is also remarked upon. One of the Old Testament's immortal lines asserts: 'The Lord is my light and my salvation; whom shall I fear?'

God's luminescence is likewise at the forefront of Islam, which declares from the very outset that the light and Allah are inextricably entwined. Allah is 'the light of the heavens and the earth,' the Koran tells us. This profound declaration is contained in a verse known as the 'Light Verse' or 'Parable of Light'. We are also informed that 'Allah guides to his light whomever he wishes.' Among his many names is 'The Light'.

The fifteenth- and early sixteenth century Islamic scholar and teacher, Al-Suyuti, also referred to the light of Allah when he described the Prophet Muhammad's journey to heaven. He pointed out how the Prophet had to place his hands over his eyes 'lest his sight be destroyed by the scintillating light of the Throne.' It was a light so bright that he despaired of ever being able to describe what he saw.

One of the great texts of Buddhism – best known in English as the Infinite Life Sūtra – likewise described this godly light. Referring to the Buddha Amitābha, we are told how 'the radiant light of all the buddhas cannot surpass the light of this buddha.'

His light radiates into every little corner of the buddha world. Among his many names are 'The Buddha of Measureless Light', 'The Buddha of Boundless Light' and 'The Buddha of Unimpeded Light'.

As we might expect, Hinduism is also suffused in celestial light. Just like Christianity, Islam and Buddhism, descriptions of deific light permeate its sacred texts. Brahma, its God of creation, is likened to 'a thunderbolt crashing throughout the heavens.' His world is characterised as 'light itself.' Another Hindu deity, Krishna, is likened to 'a mass of light shining everywhere with the radiance of flaming fire and the sun.' A further Hindu deity is named Surya or 'The Supreme Light'.

It would be remiss of me to refer to the light of God without considering the peace and love associated with it. Let us first examine the feeling of peace. It is one of the most profound sensations noted by those who find themselves in God's light. They use words like 'comforting', 'beautiful' and 'euphoric' to describe what the feeling is like. They employ phrases like 'pure joy', 'great serenity' and 'total happiness'.

One of my interviewees articulated the sensation well. 'There was a wonderful aura of peace,' Edward remarked concerning God's light. 'It was absolutely wonderful and reassuring. The only comparison I can make is with a new-born baby against its mother's breasts. It was so lovely and soft and reassuring. It was really heavenly. It felt like, "At last, I'm home." I had this experience as a teenager and yet I still remember it even though I'm in my mid-80s now; it had such an impact on me.'

The second sensation concerns the love emanating from, and surrounding, the light of God. Those who return from death say the feeling is beyond anything they encountered in life. It is warm, pleasurable and joyful; sometimes it is rapturous and ecstatic.

'I felt this incredible sense of love and warmth,' said Alan. 'In some ways, it felt like how you would feel when you'd fall in love with someone for the first time. You'd get butterflies in your heart and the top of your chest. Yet, in other ways, it was more like the old love you would feel from a parent, where everything was OK and everything was going to be OK, everything was calm and there was no badness or suffering. I just closed my eyes and felt really reassured.'

Both these emotions – the feelings of peace and love – can be found littered throughout scripture in numerous references to God. In Christianity, we see God described as 'the God of Peace' or 'the Lord of Peace' and Jesus described as 'the Prince of Peace'. The 'peace of God' surpasses all comprehension, the Bible says. Peace is also present in Hindu scripture and is at the root of Islam. Shalom, which is the Hebrew word for peace, is central to Jewish beliefs.

Scriptural references to God's love are widespread, as well. Love is referenced more than 500 times in the Bible, the exact number of citations depending on which version you read. When asked by one of the Pharisees which commandment is the greatest, Jesus replied that it is to love God, with the second greatest being to 'love your neighbour as yourself.' 'Whoever does not love does not know God, because God is love,' declared John, the Apostle.

Islam, too, is brimming with divine love. Of the 99 names given to God in Islam, one refers to him as 'The Loving One'. According to the Koran, he is 'full of loving kindness.' Buddhism may also be said to be a 'religion of love'. Its central virtues include compassion, kindness and rejoicing in other people's well-being. In Hinduism, *prem* denotes elevated love, which involves selflessness and a willingness to give without expectation of recompense.

Surprisingly, in light of what we have just seen in various religions, we find that the God of the Old Testament is far from peaceful or loving. Indeed, it would be very difficult to find a more nasty and disagreeable character. As Richard Dawkins, the renowned author and atheist, puts it in *The God Delusion*: God is 'a vindictive, bloodthirsty ethnic cleanser; a misogynistic, homophobic, racist, infanticidal, genocidal, filicidal, pestilential, megalomaniacal, sadomasochistic, capriciously malevolent bully.' Dawkins couldn't have been more pointed in his remarks.

Even a brief glance at the Old Testament bears out the truth of this assertion. Speaking to Noah, in Genesis, God tells him how he is about to 'wipe from the face of the earth every living creature I have made.' In Exodus we read how God 'struck down all the firstborn in Egypt, from the firstborn of Pharaoh, who sat on the throne, to the firstborn of the prisoner, who was in the dungeon, and the firstborn of all the livestock as well.'

In Genesis we read of God raining down 'burning sulphur' on Sodom and Gomorrah, 'destroying all those living in the cities – and also the vegetation in the land.' Lot's wife, who looked back, had the misfortune of being turned into 'a pillar of salt.' In Leviticus we are acquainted with a God who says to those who do not listen to him and are hostile to him: 'You will eat the flesh of your sons and the flesh of your daughters.'

Why God in the Old Testament should be so clouded in dark malevolence is difficult to explain, especially when the New Testament describes a God so full of brightness and light. Undoubtedly, the political atmosphere among the tribes of Israel was dark in Old Testament times, with God's 'chosen people' being constantly subjected to conflict and conquest, exile and destruction, and in particular to occupation from the empires of Persia and Rome.

Nothing could have made these Old Testament readers feel happier than to see their enemies being struck down. We see in Deuteronomy references to defeating enemies, destroying them, showing no favour to them, even not intermarrying with them, which must have warmed readers' hearts. That God would provide for 'the deliverance of Israel', using violence if needs be, was a common expectation.

Instead of this vengeful saviour along came a New Testament messiah preaching benevolence, generosity, goodwill and fraternity. 'Whoever loves God must also love his brother' must have sounded alien to Jewish ears. 'Love your enemies' must have been even more shocking. Whatever the explanation might be, the newly-described God was a lot more likeable than the one pictured in earlier times.

As we have seen in this chapter, the difficulty in describing God is common to many people who believe they have been in his presence. Most identify the sensations he represents, among them profound feelings of peace, love, goodness, kindness and compassion, while also of course sensing the wisdom and warmth that emanates from his light.

Occasionally, people will put a name or physical form to him, perhaps identifying him as Shiva, Vishnu, Jesus Christ or some other deity, depending on their religious affiliations. Yet, most often, the God they encounter occupies no physical form but is something else – something associated with light.

What exactly that 'something' might be has been alluded to by many people. What they refer to is the light of consciousness. One person spoke of experiencing God's light as 'an enormous consciousness' of which her consciousness was a part. Another person reflected that his consciousness had been 'merged with the supreme primordial consciousness.'

Yet another described God as being an amalgam of all the laws of nature, science and emotions, suggesting that 'we must all be a small part of him.' In all three cases, survival as part of a light-filled cosmic greatness was pinpointed as being at the hub of life after death. When it comes to the final chapter, we will see how uncannily insightful these people's remarks are in helping explain our final journey to the light.

In the meantime, that mystifying, enchanting, spellbinding divine light provides us with a fitting note to end this chapter. Despite all the sacred texts and ancient manuscripts, it can reasonably be said that it took *The Ten Commandments*, the movie mentioned earlier, to first describe to a mass audience what the concept of God's light was about. The director's task in illustrating not only the parting of the Red Sea but also the 'burning bush' and other light-filled images was an unenviable challenge. Having agonised over what interpretations to use, it was finally decided to stick to the descriptions outlined in the Bible.

The closing stages of the movie, as a result, have left us with some of the most celebrated and scripturally authentic images illustrating the light of God. After Moses walks back down the mountain carrying the tablets of stone, he is told: 'The light of God shines from you, Moses.' He is also informed: 'You are God's torch that lights the way to freedom.' As we might expect from an epic of this stature, he then walks towards the light rays pouring from the darkened sky. Moses is going home to the God of Light.

HOW WE IMAGINE
HEAVEN

Whoever thought up the idea of heaven being located on clouds owes us a major apology. The image is everywhere – in art, literature and poetry, on book covers and TV. Master painters, including Raphael, couldn't resist drawing chubby little angels sitting on puffy balls of cotton wool in the sky. Cherubs on clouds have appeared in commercials selling soap powder, toilet tissue and cream cheese.

Shakespeare referred to 'angels-veiling clouds' in his comedy *Love's Labour's Lost*. Dickens mentioned 'angelic messengers descending through the air on clouds like feather-beds' in *A Christmas Carol*. Wordsworth alluded to 'evening's angelic clouds' in a poem. So ingrained is the angelic cloud image that it has become the automatic point of reference of where, if we are lucky, we will end up after death.

The blame for this, it seems, rests with the prophet Daniel. Writing of a vision he had many centuries before Christ, he described how he saw the 'Son of Man' coming on 'the clouds of heaven.' This imagery was used time and again, most notably by Jesus when he told his disciples how on his eventual return people would see him 'coming on the clouds of the sky.' Although clearly intended as a metaphor, his remark was taken to suggest that those entering heaven might spend their time reclining on clouds in the company of God.

Any person who flies will know that there are no angels or saints, or even ordinary souls, living on clouds. Of course, that wasn't known by our earth-bound ancestors living before or around the time of Christ. No doubt, many looked up and conjectured – just as Daniel inferred and Jesus inadvertently implied – that their loved ones were lying on white, fluffy globes of condensation in the sky.

Mankind has always been compelled to know what heaven looks like and where it is. We want a physical, material, tangible image, something framed in terms of the world we live in. Its structures need to be real, substantial and familiar to help us understand where our loved ones have gone and where we will end up after death.

Suggestions of a glorious, noble and magnificent heaven aren't enough. Insights featuring love, peace and joy are inadequate. References to an eternal life in the company of God are unsatisfactory. What we seek is something much more clear-cut and discernible – a description of its size, shape and location, of its architecture and configuration – and that's exactly what many religions have attempted to provide.

For a man who was said to be the 'Son of God', with a father in heaven, Jesus was remarkably tight-lipped about describing the paradise we might go to after we die. He made reference to God's 'house' with its 'many mansions' or 'many rooms'. He promised his disciples he would 'prepare a place' for them there. He spoke of heaven in terms of 'eternal life' or as a 'kingdom' or 'paradise'. However, apart from identifying the rules to get there, his insights were circumspect, woolly and vague.

Insights from other ancient sources were only slightly more expansive. To begin with, our early forebears broadly agreed that heaven is somewhere up above. Perhaps because of the seemingly limitless expanse of sky, or the distant planets and stars, they believed that paradise was located on high. This was apparent in the Book of Isaiah, where God was said to live 'in a high and holy place.' It was also evident from God's remark to Moses that he had 'come down' to help his people.

Our predecessors were also interested in the actual physical 'look' of heaven. Once again, it was Moses – the prophet found abandoned as a baby in a basket on the Nile and who later walked down the mountain with the Ten Commandments – who was the first to offer us a description. He did so around 13 or 14 centuries before Christ. Following from the previous chapters, it should come as no surprise that light filled the picture he painted.

After climbing the mountain, in the midst of a cloud, Moses witnessed the Lord and the heavenly terrain he stood on. 'The glory of the Lord,' he said, 'was like a consuming fire on the mountain top.' Brightness was present in the bejewelled surface under the Lord's feet. 'A pavement of sapphire, as clear as the sky itself,' was how he described it.

This gradually-evolving picture of heaven as a place set on high, filled with light and fire, was soon added to by observations from another prophet, Ezekiel. His insights – this time dating from around the sixth century before Christ – were again dominated by light.

Ezekiel went a step further than his predecessors, describing heaven in terms of gleaming gems, precious stones, brilliant jewels and, of course, the light that emanates from them. He told us the sky was 'like the colour of an awesome crystal.' The throne was 'in appearance like a sapphire stone.'

On the throne was 'a likeness with the appearance of a man', who from the waist upwards was surrounded by fire the colour of amber and from the waist down was like 'fire with brightness all around.' This, he concluded, was 'the appearance of the likeness of the glory of the Lord.'

These heavenly features – brilliant precious stones and fire – set the stage for subsequent descriptions of heaven extending into the New Testament and right up to the present day. The two elements ultimately boil down to that single most important characteristic identified by those who temporarily die – namely, the light, with all the attendant dazzling brightness that jewels, gems and fire imply.

From the Old Testament onwards, it was as if this cardinal feature of light became written in stone. Nowhere is this more evident than in the New Testament's Book of Revelation, where we are given a detailed outline of the heavenly vision experienced by a man who was most likely the Apostle John. Not only did he witness 'a rainbow that shone like an emerald' encircling God's throne, but the one who sat there 'had the appearance of jasper and ruby.'

John also provided a light-filled view of the 24 elders who sat around God's throne. 'They were dressed in white and had crowns of gold on their heads,' he remarked. 'From the throne came flashes of lightning, rumblings and peals of thunder. In front of the throne, seven lamps were blazing. These are the seven spirits of God. Also in front of the throne there was what looked like a sea of glass, clear as crystal.'

Graphic though these images are, they pale by comparison with the physical portrayal John provided of the eternal home of the blessed that will follow the final judgement. Nothing compares to the size of this 'New Jerusalem'. Its length, breadth and height each extends to the equivalent of approximately 1,500 miles. By any standards, this would be a massive structure, reaching way beyond the earth's stratosphere and encompassing a land mass extending east from London to Helsinki and south from London to Gibraltar.

Certainly for the people in biblical times, anything this size would encompass all the land that was understood to exist. They would have had no comprehension of the Americas or Antipodes, and even less of the North and South Poles. Viewed in this way, we might speculate that the purpose of John's extravagant report was less to do with an actual outline of the city's size and more to do with emphasising its spectacular enormity and grandeur. With walls of jasper, gates of pearl and streets of pure gold, it would be a bright, dazzling edifice indeed.

This notion that light dominates the physical structures of heaven is reinforced by further references in sacred texts and in modern-day near-death accounts. According to both sets of sources, the impact of celestial translucence is pervasive and omnipresent. A brilliant lustre or glow radiates everywhere, draining all things of colour and imbuing heavenly features with a ghostly white sheen.

Even the clothes worn by deceased family or friends who come to meet new arrivals at the borders of death are affected by heaven's brightness. Sometimes the clothes appear to be washed out by the brilliance of the ambient light. Other times the light behind the figures is so intense that the colour of the clothes can't be discerned in the surrounding radiant blaze.

This sensation of sartorial brilliance, or 'whiteness', is widely reported. One woman I interviewed, who had her near-death experience during a hysterectomy, described the deceased people she had encountered as wearing 'long, white, gleaming garments,' having 'white, pale skin' and 'long, white, gleaming hair.' Another woman, who had a stroke, recalled meeting a figure 'dressed all in white.'

A man who temporarily left his body as a result of pulmonary problems explained how he came across two angelic figures 'dressed in white satin' and a figure he took to be Christ 'with silver-white hair.' Among the many other examples I encountered was a woman who saw her deceased sister wearing an unfamiliar white dress, with almost everything including her clothes and her face being white.

What is notable about these reports is that they are almost exact replicas of accounts recorded in biblical times. As far back as the Book of Revelation, written shortly after the death of Christ, we read how those who overcome their sins will 'be dressed in white.' Others who have never sinned will walk with God, 'dressed in white.' Revelation additionally portrays the great multitude surrounding the throne of God as 'wearing white robes,' no doubt reflecting the ambient brilliance.

Apart from these early biblical light-filled allusions, it was a woman-martyr named Vibia Perpetua who, at the beginning of the third century, provided us with the first genuinely popular description of heaven. Her story was remarkable for a number of reasons. To begin with, it was the work of a woman, written by herself and in her own name; in that sense, it was the first of its kind.

Just as important, Perpetua's martyrdom ended up being well-documented, taking place at the arena in Carthage in 203 AD. Her self-penned text, written while still in prison, was widely distributed throughout the Christian community from the third century onwards and was read to gatherings of the faithful. It had an enormous impact in hammering home the concept of a physical place we go to after death.

The story behind Perpetua's martyrdom is both fascinating and gruesome. She came from a noble background, was well-educated, and had adopted the Christian faith of her mother while rejecting the pagan beliefs of her father. At the age of 22, she was arrested under the persecutions of Emperor Severus. Sentenced to die, she was brought to the arena where she was at first savaged by a wild animal and then put to the sword.

Her prison diary, which survived her, revealed some of the earliest insights to the physical structure of heaven. First, she explained how in a vision prior to her death she ascended to heaven on 'a ladder of tremendous height made of bronze.' Notably, this journey took place upwards. What she then outlined was remarkable.

'I saw an immense garden, and in it a grey-haired man sat in shepherd's garb; tall he was, and milking sheep,' Perpetua wrote. 'And standing around him were many thousands of people clad in white garments. He raised his head, looked at me, and said: "I am glad you have come, my child."

'He called me over to him and gave me, as it were, a mouthful of the milk he was drawing; and I took it into my cupped hands and consumed it. And all those who stood around said: "Amen!" At the sound of this word I came to, with the taste of something sweet still in my mouth.'

Short though this account is, Perpetua's text reassured fellow Christians that not only did a physical heaven exist but there was a God there along with 'many thousands' of people, most probably deceased family and friends. For those whose religious convictions were wavering, they could now rest easier in the knowledge that they would live on after death in a specific place and in the company of others and of God.

Perpetua's account was also interesting for its references to a heavenly garden and a shepherd looking after his sheep. The shepherd, of course, was the figurative representation of God caring for his flock. The milk was the potion that would fortify Perpetua during her trials ahead. It was the garden, however, that was of particular interest in that it identified an alternative view of heaven to accompany the shimmering jewel-encrusted cities evoked up to then.

Numerous similar heavenly descriptions involving gardens or rustic landscapes have been included in visionary and near-death accounts since Perpetua wrote her story nearly two millennia ago. They involve wonderful landscapes filled with rich green fields, gently-flowing streams and vibrantly-coloured flowers. Bathed in summer light, the scenes are warm and welcoming, tranquil and serene. Sweet aromas are everywhere. Peace reigns supreme.

In obvious ways, these rustic depictions are entirely different from the light-filled images described earlier. Stand back from them, however, and you will notice the underlying characteristic they share in common – they each describe a glorious, welcoming, peaceful destination, full of tranquillity and warmth; the sort of place where everyone would want to be. What better definition can one find of heaven?

A typical example concerns a woman named Antoinette, who haemorrhaged having lost her baby boy in childbirth. 'I could literally feel the life going out of me,' she recalled. Having left her body, she soon found herself in a tunnel full of white, bright light.

'I was floating down the tunnel,' Antoinette told me. 'It was like I was on a bed, face forward. I was there for a while. I wanted to keep going and I wanted to get to the end of the tunnel. There was a door at the end, which was half-open. The door was light coloured as well.

'Beyond the door was a garden. It was absolutely beautiful. Everything was very lush and coloured green. It was also full of lovely, coloured flowers. The flowers had colours like red and yellow. It was a place you would want to go to, a place you would want to be in.

'There was a bridge in the garden, which you could go up on and walk over. There were bars along the side of the bridge and there was a trickle of water under it. The water was like a little river going through the flowers.

'The big thing I remember was trying to get through the door. I wondered, "Will I make it there?" All I wanted to do was just get into the garden. I just wanted to get to this place. I desperately wanted to be there.'

Similar lush terrain was identified in the 1890s by Rebecca Ruter Springer, who became unwell and temporarily died. Having left her body, she travelled to a glorious place full of 'perfect grass and flowers.' There were wonderful trees there, 'whose drooping branches were laden with exquisite blossoms and fruits of many kinds.'

Rebecca continued: 'The grass and flowers looked as though fresh-washed by summer showers, and not a single blade was any colour but the brightest green. The air was soft and balmy, though invigorating; and instead of sunlight there was a golden and rosy glory everywhere.

'Beneath the trees, in many happy groups, were little children, laughing and playing, running hither and thither in their joy, and catching in their tiny hands the bright-winged birds that flitted in and out among them, as though sharing in their sports, as they doubtless were.

'All through the grounds, older people were walking, sometimes in groups, sometimes by twos, sometimes alone, but all with an air of peacefulness and happiness that made itself felt by even me, a stranger. All were in spotless white, though many wore about them or carried in their hands clusters of beautiful flowers.'

These balmy pastoral scenes present a soothing, blissful interpretation of heaven, reminding us of worry-free, sunny summer days, with gentle breezes, rich terrain and wonderful feelings of happiness and joy. Gentle rivers flow through the landscape. Everyone is calm and at peace. Life is carefree and warm.

Interestingly, Islam describes an equally serene, warm, rustic heaven, full of splendour and luxury, with greenery and light. Only the finest of everything is there – 'beautiful mansions in gardens of everlasting bliss', rivers whose 'mud is musk and its water is whiter than milk', a land with 'soil of saffron' and 'pebbles of pearl and sapphire', a Paradise where people live 'in peace and security' in an 'eternal abode of radiant joy.'

A bright sheen is everywhere, reflecting the brilliance of Allah. Everything is startlingly bright. We are told how 'the trunks of the trees are gold', no doubt shimmering in the light. Bricks are said to be made of 'gold and silver.' The women have beautiful, big and lustrous eyes. Those who witness Allah are 'shining, radiant.' In other words, the ambiance is brilliant, magnificent, dazzling, creating a joyful atmosphere for those who are there.

Similar to what we have seen in Christianity – especially in the vision of John – some features of Islam's Paradise are also exaggerated in size. There are tents which are 60 miles high and, some reports say, 60 miles wide. Some trees are so big that even trying to imagine them 'makes one's head spin.' One type of tree has leaves 'like the ears of elephants.' Another tree's shadow takes 100 years to cross. Nothing in this life could ever compare to wonders like that!

Right up to the present day, narratives from monks, knights, noblemen, theologians and ordinary people have reproduced the main images of heaven seen so far in this chapter. They have spanned many world religions, including Christianity, but non-religious people have told their stories, too. At their core, the images have described either lush green pastoral settings or shimmering cities, with God at their centre. Familiar souls – including deceased family, former acquaintances and friends – are present. Underlying all is the light, with its associated sensations of peace, love and joy.

One well-known exposition, chronicled in the very late twelfth century, conforms to the norm, especially in its description of a crystal-like structure and the presence of light. The account comes from England, from a man identified as 'The Monk of Evesham', who was discovered dead by his fellow friars following a long illness.

'When they found that he had lost all pulse in his veins for some time, they cried out altogether that he was dead,' we are told. He soon revived and recalled what had occurred. He said that, accompanied by 'an old man clothed in white garments,' he was taken on a tour of the afterlife.

'I saw what appeared to be a wall of crystal that was so high that no one could look over it and so long that there appeared to be no end,' the monk recollected. 'When we approached it, I saw it glittered with a most noble shining brightness from within....let no one ask me how glittering was the inconceivable brightness or how strong was the light....I am not able to express this in words, not even to recollect it in my mind.'

A further insight to heaven – this time from the thirteenth century – is also notable. The account comes from an Englishman named Thurkill, who lived in London. We are told that he left his body and, accompanied by a guide, was shown 'certain things that are hidden from men and women in the flesh.' Among the places he saw was a temple containing the blessed. The vision occurred in late October 1206.

'There he saw in white apparel many of both sexes whom he had seen in life,' we are informed. 'They were climbing up to the temple and enjoying great happiness. The further the spirits climbed up the steps of the temple, the more white and shining they became.

'In that great church he saw many very beautiful mansions. In them dwelt the spirits of the just, whiter than snow. Their faces and crowns glittered like golden light. At certain hours of each day they heard songs from heaven, as if all kinds of music were sounding in harmonious melody. This soothed and refreshed all the inhabitants of the temple by its agreeable softness.'

Another report is worth noting, if only because it came from the mouth of a child – and children are known for their honesty and accuracy in describing near-death accounts. The child in question was a Californian girl named Daisy, who died on 8 October 1864 from bilious fever. Aged around ten years at the time of her illness, she effectively lived in both worlds – here and in the afterlife – as she approached her death.

Her remarks were most insightful regarding the 'mansions' of heaven. Contrary to the frequently-quoted references that there are physical structures in paradise, she pointed out that she saw no such things during her visits there. She was responding to a neighbour who had read the well-known Bible passage to her: 'Let not your heart be troubled. In my Father's house are many mansions. I go to prepare a place for you.'

Daisy interjected: 'Mansions, that means houses. I don't see real houses there; but there is what would be places to meet each other in....Perhaps the Testament tells about mansions so we will feel we are going to have a home in heaven, and perhaps when I get there I'll find a home. And if I do, the heavenly flowers and trees that I love so much here, for I do see them, and that they are more beautiful than anything you could imagine, they will be there.'

Daisy's story – one of a long succession of accounts recorded down through the ages and quite a distance from the first heavenly reports of biblical times – brings us to within a century-and-a-half of today. Little has changed over the years, with many of today's near-death descriptions replicating what has been said before. Physical images may be much less commonly reported than light images, but they are recalled and, to those who perceive them, they do exist.

Whether or not these golden gates, golden pavements or buildings constructed of wonderful gemstones are present in paradise we can only wait and see. Alternatively, whether there are idyllic, green, grassy, verdant heavenly pastures we also won't know until we pass to the other side. Only in time will these things be revealed.

In the meantime, we might ask whether the images are meant to be tangible – instead, perhaps they are just representations to help us understand the glory and magnificence of what we face after death. The fragrant odours and pleasant green meadows may be mere metaphors for the indescribable wonders we will encounter. The crowns and bricks of gold, precious stones and blazing lamps may merely illustrate the light that we will see.

That might well explain the reticence and dearth of clarity, described earlier, that Jesus demonstrated in his references to heaven. He may have realised that the heavenly state is non-material, non-physical, beyond easy description or popular comprehension. To use a phrase from Corinthians, he might have known that because it is a place or state which 'no eye has seen' or 'no ear has heard' or 'no human mind has conceived', it is therefore beyond our grasp.

Perhaps he ultimately understood that heaven is less to do with a physical place and more to do with a post-death state of supreme, definitive happiness, where our consciousness creates its own reality and where all our hopes and wishes are realised. This proposition will be examined in the final chapter of this book.

THE PEOPLE WE MEET IN
HEAVEN

Everybody will be 33 years of age in heaven! That strange notion derives from a proposition dating back to the Middle Ages. The proposition was no flippant piece of conjecture but resulted from ideas put forward by two leading Church thinkers – Peter Lombard, the Bishop of Paris whose *Four Books of Sentences* became the great theological text of his era; and St. Thomas Aquinas, another prominent theologian of the age and author of *Summa Theologica*.

Underlying the suggestion was some diligent detective work to find out what age Jesus was when he died. Biblical clues were identified, the most important being a reference in Luke stating that 'Jesus, when he began his ministry, was about thirty years of age.' When combined with information from John telling us that Jesus attended three Passovers during his ministry, which ended with his crucifixion, it was deduced that he must have been aged 33 at the time of his death.

So what about the rest of us being 33 year-olds in heaven? The case is crystal clear, we are informed. It is all down to Paul in his Epistle to the Philippians, written a few decades after Christ died, telling us that in heaven God will transform our ordinary bodies so that they will be like Christ's 'glorified body.' From there on, the logic is simple: if Jesus was 33 at the time of his death and resurrection – the time when his body was 'glorified' – then, so be it, that's the same age we will all be in heaven.

This choice of age is perceived to be justified medically as it describes a time of life when people's physical and intellectual capacities may be said to have peaked while the slow decline into old age is just about to begin. To use a phrase employed by St. Thomas Aquinas, it is an age when 'the movement of growth is terminated, and from which the movement of degeneration begins.'

The age also has implications for the general atmosphere in heaven – no crying babies; no troublesome teenagers; no cranky old folk; no geriatricians and very few rheumatologists; and no need for an old-age pension! In their place would be the fittest, healthiest, most intellectually-active group of 30 year-olds collected together in the prime of their afterlife!

There are problems, however. It is one thing to suggest that old people, with their infirmities and age-related imperfections, might revert to being sprightly 33 year-olds, and be happy to do so. It is a greater challenge, by far, to explain how babies, children or adolescents might suddenly advance to their 30s. They would just do so, please don't ask why, Peter Lombard unconvincingly tells us, while stressing that even the tiniest baby would have the same age as the rest of us in heaven.

There are other problems with the age of 33, too. As with many biblical issues, theologians differ in their interpretation of the age Jesus was when he died. Some experts, including Peter Lombard, speculated that he might have been only 30 and not 33 at the time of his death. More wondered whether age would be relevant at all, given the realm we were supposedly entering.

What most Bible scholars neglected, however, was to examine the sizeable, and much more meaningful, evidence provided by people who have undergone near-death experiences. In sharp contrast to the speculation of theologians, the conclusions to be drawn from their stories are definitive and clear – namely, that all age ranges are represented in heaven.

This is certainly true of reports from the more than 100 survivors of near-death experiences I have interviewed, many of whom described meeting deceased family and friends at the dividing line between this life and the next. These deceased former loved ones ranged in age from recently-born babies who died shortly after birth to old grandparents who passed away years earlier.

These known and well-loved relatives and friends are said to await the arrival of people who have just died. They always look happy, healthy and well, and are pleased to see their old acquaintances. They include dead parents, children, brothers, sisters, other near and distant relatives and former close friends, reflecting the broad span of age ranges encountered in real life.

They all look better than ever. Previous injuries or deformities have disappeared. People who died in traumatic road accidents have their pre-crash features restored. Those who passed away from cancer no longer bear the worn, tired, sickly look they had before death. Victims who had died from other traumatic incidents also look their best. All reports indicate that, whatever our physical state prior to death, we will look our finest in heaven.

Pamela's father is a case in point. He died from cancer, with the primary disease being located in his chest cavity and some secondary disease existing elsewhere. He had a very bad death, Pamela remarked. Later, having faced death herself during a troublesome childbirth, she departed her body. Having entered a tunnel of light, she encountered her dead father.

'He looked exactly as he was when he was healthy,' Pamela recalled. 'He had looked terrible when he died; he had lost so much weight. But when I saw him, he looked like he did when he was well. He was there, dressed in shirt and slacks, just like he was before he was sick. He was so happy and he was smiling.

'He was walking towards me and I was walking towards him. I knew immediately by his walk that it was my father. He came closer and closer. He got to a distance where I could reach my hand out to touch him. I wanted to go with him. However, he reached his left hand out towards me, with the palm up, as if to say stop.

'He shook his head and smiled reassuringly at me. I heard the words, "Not yet!" He then just vanished. At that second, I was straight back to where I had been beforehand. About ten minutes later, my son was born. I was disappointed afterwards. If I could have been back with my father, I would have gone.'

Tom's father also died following a battle with cancer yet looked perfect in heaven. The era in which he contracted the disease was an early one, characterised by relatively primitive, unsophisticated treatments and little chance of survival. It was pointed out to me that the father had died 'a worn man, drawn, with nothing left of him and his face shrivelled.'

Thirty years later, Tom had a heart attack and temporarily died. Having left his body, he could see the doctors working on him below. They were saying, 'He's gone! He's gone! He's gone!' At that point, he floated down a tunnel and headed towards what he described as 'a massive setting sun.' The light drew him towards it. Then, straight in front of him, out of nowhere, his father appeared.

Despite his father's harrowing death, he looked perfect – 'like a man of 20,' as Tom put it. Although his face had looked emaciated before he died, it now looked healthy and fresh. Tom said he 'never saw him in his life so good.' His father then extended his arms and embraced Tom, calling out his name. He said, 'Your time isn't up yet. You've got to go back.' No sooner had he said that than Tom was back again in his body.

Interestingly, the promise that disabilities, injuries and other impairments no longer exist in heaven – reflecting what you have just read – is clearly articulated in the Bible. It is beautifully expressed in the Book of Isaiah, which was written around eight centuries before Christ. Extraordinarily accurate in its prophecies, this book of the Old Testament is regarded as one of the most important of all biblical texts.

Isaiah reveals how, after Christ eventually arrives to establish his kingdom, all will be transformed for those who may be infirm. Disabilities and deformities will disappear. 'Then will the eyes of the blind be opened, and the ears of the deaf unstopped. Then will the lame leap like a deer, and the mute tongue shout for joy,' is how the text puts it. Followers of Islam are also instructed that those who enter Paradise will have 'the most perfect and beautiful form,' free from infirmity, blindness or any other handicap.

St. Augustine, in his book *The City of God*, also touches on the topic. Addressing the state of resurrected bodies, this fourth- and fifth-century theologian describes how 'the body shall be of that size which it either had attained or should have attained in the flower of its youth, and shall enjoy the beauty that arises from preserving symmetry and proportion in all its members.'

Augustine goes on to offer the strangest explanation of how imperfections disappear; so strange it is worth noting. If there is any deformity in the body, he said, it will be redistributed throughout the rest of the body so it will no longer be noticeable.

As a result, the general stature of the body will be 'somewhat increased by the distribution in all the parts of that which, in one place, would have been unsightly.' How a severe weight problem, where the weight is already uniformly spread, would be dealt with, he never explains.

Undeterred by any flaws in his theory, Augustine concluded that after we die there will be 'no deformity, no infirmity, no languor, no corruption, nothing of any kind which would ill become that kingdom in which the children of the resurrection and of the promise shall be equal to the angels of God, if not in body and age, at least in happiness.'

Quite apart from such theological musings, what is clear is that we *will* meet again our close loved ones in heaven. They will have no uncertainty about who we are. We will have no doubts about who they are, either. In short, they will be known to us and we will be known to them. To put it another way, our personal identities will be retained.

This retention of our personal identities, or individuality, is unequivocally stated in the Book of Job – probably the oldest text in the Bible – where Job looks ahead to his afterlife with God. After his 'skin has been destroyed,' he says, 'in my flesh I will see God; I myself will see him with my own eyes – I, and not another.' Another biblical text – the Book of Isaiah – quotes the Lord as saying: 'As the new heavens and the new earth that I make will endure before me, so will your name and descendants endure.'

After the resurrection, Jesus too appeared not as some ghost-like figure but as himself. 'Why are you troubled?' he asks his disciples, who are frightened when he suddenly appears. 'See my hands and my feet, that it is I myself. Touch me and see.

For a spirit does not have flesh and bones as you see that I have.'
All three biblical excerpts, just referred to, reveal the extent to
which the essence of our earthly selves survives after death.

The inference from this is clear – couples who were joined
together on earth will recognise each other and meet again in
heaven. This is validated by my personal research. Dead parents,
grandparents and parents-in-law, standing side by side, featured
in many near-death accounts described to me over the years.
They materialised at the border between life and death, where
they awaited the arrival of their newly-dead offspring. They
always looked happy and were comfortable in each other's
company.

Catherine's near-death experience illustrates this point well.
Having headed to the light after becoming seriously ill, she saw
her deceased parents together with a dead brother. They were
waiting for her at the end of a tunnel, in what she described as
a 'soft light.' They were happy, comfortable and glad to see her
arriving.

'They looked exactly the same as they were before they
died,' Catherine said. 'They hadn't aged. They were happier
and not stressed like they used to be in this world. Everyone, I
suppose, has difficulties in this life, but they didn't have them
in their world. They were smiling at me, but they never said
anything.

'I felt very happy, content and glad to see them. It was a
really nice experience. Initially, I wanted to go to them. But I
suddenly felt I wasn't ready. I didn't want to leave because of
my children and my husband. I also wasn't ready to leave this
world as I had more to do. I had one foot just beyond the
halfway mark, but I didn't go any further. Instead, I came back
and back.'

We will likewise meet and converse with deceased *extended* family members in paradise. The Old Testament tells us that Abraham, having died at a 'good old age,' was 'gathered to his people' – in other words, reunited with his extended family who had predeceased him. The identical phrase – 'gathered to his people' – was used to explain what happened to Isaac, Ishmael and Jacob after they passed away.

The Roman philosopher Cicero, who lived from 106 – 43 BC, wrote that he hoped to meet not extended family but a broad collection of former beloved friends among a 'divine congregation of departed spirits.' The Greek philosopher Socrates, who lived from 469 – 399 BC, spoke of a similar place we go to after death which is 'inhabited by the spirits of departed men.' In England, the seventh- and eighth-century monk and scholar Bede wrote how his fellow monk Drythelm met 'many companies of happy people' during his visit to the otherworld.

Meetings with non-immediate family members or friends after death, endorsing what you have just read, also featured in many of the case histories I have encountered. The figures were occasionally hard to recognise. Despite this, the people I spoke to said they were still sure they knew who they were. Many instantly deduced they were long-lost relatives who, despite not being identifiable, emerged to make contact after death.

'There were three old people coming towards me, walking along in a purposeful way,' Sarah, who experienced this phenomenon, recollected. 'I didn't know them and I couldn't say they were anybody in particular. They definitely weren't my grandparents because I knew them – unless this was the body they have in the next world.

'I wanted to go to them as if they were long-lost relatives or ancestors or friends or something. It was an overwhelming desire.

They were familiar to me and I would have trusted them and felt close to them. I definitely felt a great empathy with them. It was an extraordinary feeling.

'Although they weren't hurrying, I was hurrying and I had a great feeling of joy. I was delighted to see them. They seemed delighted to see me, too. There was an affinity between us and I knew they were mine and I was meant to be with them. This was nirvana. I was so anxious to go to them and I didn't want to come back.'

Sometimes, even though the deceased relatives are unknown, it is clear what era they came from. This is ascertainable from the style of clothes they wear. Although the clothes are normally of little concern to people who temporarily die – concerned, as they are, with bigger matters – they occasionally note them and recall what they were like.

A group of between 25 and 30 people dressed in clothes from the early 1900s greeted one young teenager who temporarily died in 1968. He travelled to the light following a terrifying near-drowning. Although he knew that the people he saw were there to greet him, he was unable to recognise them. They gave him a warm welcome.

'They were wearing clothes not from 1968 but from a long time before that, maybe the early 1900s,' Frank recalled. 'Most of them were dressed in black, both women and men. They were standing around in a semicircle. Their lips were moving, so I knew they were talking, although I couldn't hear any words or hear their voices. I couldn't hear what they were saying.

'I just knew they were there to greet me, although I didn't recognise any of them. I definitely knew they were there for me. They looked like ordinary people and I knew they knew me. I knew I had some connection with them. I felt they were related to me in some way and I felt really wanted. I'm convinced they were my dead relations.'

This feature of deceased relatives wearing era-specific clothes was likewise described to me by a woman named Mary. Having experienced a miscarriage in the 1990s, she encountered her husband's dead grandparents. Although she had never met them, she immediately knew who they were. They, too, were dressed in clothes they would have worn at the time they were alive.

'They were dressed in clothes of their era,' Mary remembered. 'The grandfather was wearing a sort of serge-style gabardine coat. I later discovered it related to work he had done at one stage in his life. His wife wore a fawn-coloured raincoat and a coloured scarf.

'They came to me. It was as though I was welcoming them into my home. They didn't stay. It was only like I was meeting them. Although I referred to what took place as a dream, it was different from that. I really felt I was there, in a different place. I was feeling and talking. I could see all around me. It wasn't just me looking at something; I was in the experience.

'About a week after it happened, I was given a gift which included a photograph of the grandfather. It was exactly as I had seen him. The grandfather was the only one of the two grandparents in it. He was working in the garden. The image of him coming to me was identical. I saw a photograph of the grandmother, years later, and she was the same, too.'

It is further reported that light may surround those we meet in heaven. Given the all-pervasive nature of heaven's brightness, this is hardly surprising. It is no shock, then, to discover that some people who arrive at the gateway to heaven meet deceased relatives who are bathed in light.

One example involves Sheila who, having died temporarily as a young child, saw her deceased grandfather silhouetted in light. She met him in what she described as a nice, bright place, full of wonderful flowers. Her grandfather was surrounded by light. Although it was bright, it was not blinding or glaring.

'There was a man there, with brightness around him,' Sheila recalled. 'He was a grandfather of mine who had died a couple of weeks before I was born. He had a moustache and he was smiling at me. He had a tweed coat on him, with a flower attached to his lapel, and he looked nice. He said, "You can't come in here yet! You can't come in here until you are as old as Granny!" I eventually came back to my body.'

In a further example, Frances explained how she saw figures standing in a field located behind what she described as a 'big, white, bright light.' She should have been blinded by the brightness of it but, as happens in almost all such cases, she wasn't. Instead, the light was comforting. 'I was so, so happy, beyond anything I could describe,' she said. She felt she was in heaven.

It is worth noting briefly that the light references in both these cases tie in with remarks in the Bible. The following are just a few relevant examples: 'The righteous will shine like the sun in the kingdom of their Father'; 'Those who are wise will shine like the brightness of the heavens'; 'Like the jewels of a crown they shall shine on his land.' These references clearly indicate that those who have entered heaven may be seen in brilliant light.

The issue of whether we age in heaven is outside the remit of people who have undergone near-death experiences. The reason is that, having arrived at the borders of death, they are separated from their deceased loved ones by a dividing line or partition and, as a result, cannot ask them. Not until they have crossed the barrier is speech or physical interaction possible. Furthermore, they rarely have a second near-death experience and are not in a position to spot changes in physical appearance.

Ancient religious texts colour in the gaps in our knowledge, indicating clearly that the physical decline of the body is not a feature of paradise. To the contrary, these texts argue, once the human body dies its new form is immortal and incorruptible.

St. Paul, in particular, articulates this view in his First Epistle to the Corinthians, written a few decades after the death of Christ. The text – which contains wonderful phrases such as 'through a glass darkly', 'all things to all men' and 'without love, I am nothing' – also refers to what our bodies will be like in heaven.

In Corinthians, St. Paul states that our new bodies will be immortal. While our old bodies are corruptible, our new bodies will be incorruptible. Our new bodies will also be glorified and spiritual. 'The dead will be raised imperishable,' he concludes, 'and we will be changed.' This concept of our being immortal in the 'Gardens of Eternity' is also present in Islam.

Whether we will meet with, and engage with, angels in heaven is unclear. In the Bible, they are not generally presented as spiritual beings who share heavenly delights with deceased souls. Instead, they are assigned very specific roles – as messengers of God, protectors of God's children, and as celestial beings whose job is to surround and worship God. They will also be God's emissaries when the Second Coming takes place.

It has been described, however, how God's angels sometimes appear to, and meet, those who undergo near-death experiences.

One interviewee of mine, Tom, outlined how his grandmother witnessed angels on her death-bed. 'I won't be with you long,' she told him. 'The angels came to me during the night. They took me to a place and showed me where I'm going to be going.'

Another interviewee, Teresa, who had a near-death experience after becoming ill during a stressful time in her life, described what she saw: 'I could see three people dressed in white. They were completely white. I couldn't see their faces. I thought they were angels. There could have been more there, I don't know, but all I saw were the three. Everything was snow white, like a big ball of snow.'

Further evidence bolstering the case that we will meet angels in heaven was provided by St. Fursa, the Irish monk who lived in the seventh century. In 633, having fallen ill, he temporarily died and saw angelic choirs and heard them singing. Sir William Barrett, the eminent physicist and author, chronicled additional cases in the late nineteenth- and early twentieth century where young people witnessed angels shortly before their deaths.

Other important heavenly inhabitants – saints – have also been encountered during afterlife journeys. In the Middle Ages, the Irish knight and nobleman Tundale, after he collapsed and temporarily died, described how he saw choirs of saints, dressed in brilliant white, singing their praises to God. Many other encounters with deceased saints – including St. Gerard and St. Michael – have been described to me in the course of my investigations.

If there is a common denominator underpinning the anecdotal accounts detailed throughout this chapter, along with the scriptural references that are also cited, it is that we will all meet again after we die. Our deceased loved ones will recognise us and we will recognise them, and we will all be reunited at the borders of death. There, as Islam puts it, we will engage in 'mutual enquiry', which will bring joy to our hearts.

Those we meet there will be those we want to meet, not those from our past who we might wish to avoid. Among all the near-death survivors I have interviewed, there has never been an unhappy encounter; nor have I come across any in the literature. Instead, the evidence points to reunions with people we were once close to, who are happy to meet us and who we are equally happy to reacquaint ourselves with after we die. It is they who will help us in our passage to the other side.

Why this should be so is worth speculating upon. It might be because, at the time of death, it is we who are ultimately responsible for what happens next – it is we who create our own reality and who shape our ultimate destiny, and it is our consciousness that determines who of the people we once knew we will encounter once we pass to the other side. This chapter, however, is no place for this discussion; instead, the discussion will be left until the final chapter of this book.

In the meantime, it seems appropriate to conclude with the story of a man who, as he approached death in his 90s, was visited by his deceased sister Mary who had passed away as a young child from the ravages of TB. In his final days, the man described how, even after nine decades, she had come to him and was looking after him. They remembered each other, and recognised each other, despite the long span of time that had elapsed.

'He seemed delighted to know she was there,' Margaret, his friend and carer, told me. 'He was very happy and pleased that she had come. And you could see that he knew perfectly well that he was the only person who could see her. To me, it was wonderful to think that after all that length of time she would remember him.

'For the rest of us, even after a short time, we forget most of the people we have known. But Mary was there as he was dying and he knew her and recognised her. She was the same as when she left; she never got old. And she came for her brother, no doubt saying, "Don't worry, I'm here!" I thought it was lovely. He died about a week after that.'

THE LIFESTYLE IN HEAVEN

There is a wonderful cartoon illustrating the potential boredom of heaven. Two inhabitants adorned with wings and halos sit on a cloud, looking completely fed up. One is bent forward, his arms crossed; the other one uses his right arm to support his head while his left hand hangs limply across his knee.

Both figures look utterly downbeat and dispirited. They really should be yawning. The second frame of the cartoon depicts a third winged inhabitant, who is listless and lethargic, as if trapped in the depths of depression. He delivers the punchline – 'Wish I'd brought a magazine.'

The cartoon – one of Gary Larson's *The Far Side* creations – gives rise to a worrying thought. For those of us used to the fast-paced, frenetic activities of earthly life, with its excitement, variety and bustle, might it just be the case that life in paradise could be deadly dull? Relaxing on a cloud while basking in sunshine sounds like a good short-term idea, but being asked to do it for eternity might be stretching things too far!

At first sight, the Bible doesn't give us much reassurance – unless, of course, you are part of a choral group, church choir, a professional crooner, background vocalist in a band, or you simply love warbling in the bath. Because heaven, we are told, is full of singing. There are massed choirs and small choirs delivering psalms, madrigals and hymns of praise to beat the band. Indeed, one might be forgiven for thinking of heaven as a happy sing-along that goes on to eternity!

We will certainly be in good musical company. Solomon, who the Bible tells us wrote 'a thousand and five' songs, will be there. David, who sang to the Lord after being delivered from his enemies, will be there, too. Even the singers who were deemed to be tax-exempt some four centuries before Christ for performing in the 'house of God' should be there, recovering after their tax-free exertions on earth.

There will be lots of musicians there, too. Trumpets, flutes, cymbals, horns, lyres, pipes, tambourines, zithers and, of course, plenty of harps are among the instruments they will be playing – and that's only some of those mentioned in the Bible. The many musicians who heralded the delivery of the Ark of the Covenant to Jerusalem – the cymbal-, harp- and lyre-playing Asaph, Heman, Jeduthun and their sons and relations, along with the 120 priests who played trumpets – will presumably be there, also.

There are no biblical references to Fender, Rickenbacker or Gibson guitar players in heaven, although no doubt they too will be present. They might, at first, feel uncomfortable in the company of their earlier counterparts dressed in robes with their rams' horns, timbrels, psalteries and sistra, all of which are mentioned in sacred texts. Perhaps they will collectively drum up some of the 'joyful noise' that we are told gives 'praise and thanks to the Lord.'

These biblical depictions of a music- and song-filled heaven may not be too far off the mark, according to at least some people who have undergone near-death experiences. Although they don't always report seeing heaven's inhabitants singing or playing their instruments, they certainly mention hearing the sweet sounds of celestial music. Occasionally, they also witness who is playing it.

Jackie is one of a handful of people I interviewed who fall into this latter category. Following a difficult childbirth, she headed through a tunnel that was lit by 'a bright, dazzling light.' Emerging into a beautiful garden, she saw angels who played musical instruments and sang. She also met her deceased grandparents, who instructed her to go back.

'There was this beautiful garden,' she told me. 'The grass was so green. On the left, three angels were playing harps and singing. The music was gorgeous. To the right of the garden was this grey stone house with a brown door. It was like a church, but it really was a mansion. It looked medieval. The sky was blue and the sun was shining.

'My grandparents came out of the house and they met me. My grandfather had died of throat cancer; my grandmother from lung cancer. They looked very well. They were very happy to see me and they gave me a big hug. I wanted to go into the house with them, but they said it wasn't my time and that I should go back and take care of my son. I floated down and came back inside myself. The next thing, I woke up.'

There is another interesting facet to Jackie's grandparents' story – it seems they were fortunate to have been married before entering heaven. The reason is simple – there is no marriage in paradise! Nor, by deduction, are there any people employed in the administrative or ceremonial end of the wedding business. At least we learn this from the response by Jesus to a troublesome piece of questioning by a Jewish sect known as the Sadducees.

The Sadducees raised a thorny issue in the hope of catching Jesus out. They first mentioned how Moses had said that if a man dies without having children his brother must marry the widow and produce offspring on his behalf. What happens then, they asked, if there are seven brothers and they all marry the widow, one by one, after each of the previous brothers dies childless? When the widow dies, of the seven whose wife will she be?

The answer given by Jesus was unequivocal. He pointed out that in heaven people 'neither marry nor be given in marriage,' thus implying that the widow wouldn't be betrothed to any of the seven. We don't know whether the response satisfied the Sadducees, but it certainly clarified that we won't be getting married if we are fortunate enough to enter paradise.

This pronouncement by Jesus, of course, simply states that marriage is not a feature of heaven; it does not state that earthly spouses won't be reunited with their former loved ones. In fact, it certainly seems from another comment made by Jesus about marriage – 'What therefore God has joined together, let not man put asunder' – that couples united by marriage on earth will continue to be couples in heaven, should they so wish.

The Koran likewise mentions how righteous believers join with their spouses, among other family members, in Paradise. It specifically outlines how spouses meet together 'in pleasant shade, on thrones reclining.' This central text of Islam additionally tells us how those reaching Paradise talk to each other. 'Some of them draw near unto others, mutually questioning,' we are informed.

Looking after our loved ones down on earth may well be an additional activity assigned to us in heaven. Those who support this proposition often point to a reference in the Epistle to the Hebrews which states that 'since we are surrounded by so great a cloud of witnesses, let us also lay aside every weight, and sin which clings so closely, and let us run with endurance the race that is set before us.'

This reference to being 'surrounded' by 'so great a cloud of witnesses' has been taken to imply that we are looked after by those who have passed on before us. Some commentators, however, argue that this interpretation may read too much into the biblical remark and that it merely refers to earthly witnesses and not to those of a celestial kind.

An additional biblical reference, seen in the Gospel of Luke, supports the view that our heavenly departed may indeed take care of us from afar. This reference specifies that 'there will be more rejoicing in heaven over one sinner who repents than over ninety-nine righteous persons who do not need to repent.' It can be reasonably deduced from this remark that those who do the rejoicing must be aware of what is happening on earth, thus bolstering the argument that not only are we observed by former loved ones but that they are actively involved in caring for us, as well.

Further evidence, of an anecdotal nature, supporting the notion that deceased loved ones look after their relatives down on earth, has come to light through my research. One woman, Johanna, spoke of how her father was looked after by a deceased close friend as he was dying in 2007. 'He was smiling at the time,' she told me. 'He said, "Christy has come to see me," which was strange because Christy had died in 1999. When I heard about what he said I thought, "Christy is going to look after my dad from here on in." I think my dad felt safe after what he saw.'

Another interviewee, Phil, explained how she received a visit from her deceased brother shortly after she had a heart attack. 'I felt my brother's presence,' she said regarding the strange sensation she experienced while being brought to hospital by ambulance. 'When I was in the ambulance it was like he was there touching me and saying "You're alright now. Don't worry. You're going to be fine."

'It was like he was holding my right hand and was standing beside me. I could really feel him. He was with me the whole way to the hospital. I felt he was with me the whole time in the hospital. I felt he was holding my hand as I was going in to surgery. I knew he was protecting me.'

Had Phil been unfortunate enough to die, she and her brother undoubtedly would have feasted together in paradise – or so we are told. Plentiful amounts of food would have been on offer. Numerous biblical references indicate this. The Book of Isaiah describes how 'the Lord Almighty will prepare a feast of rich food for all peoples, a banquet of aged wine the best of meats and the finest of wines.'

Additional culinary references are featured in the Gospel of Luke, where we hear of heavenly inhabitants who 'eat at the feast in the kingdom of God.' These delights are so lavish for souls entering heaven that 'never again will they hunger; never again will they thirst.'

Dining companions will match the quality of the food. In Matthew, we are told how the elect 'will take their places at the feast with Abraham, Isaac and Jacob.' Better still, Luke quotes Jesus as remarking, 'You may eat and drink at my table in my kingdom and sit on thrones, judging the twelve tribes of Israel.'

The Koran likewise reassures us that there will be copious supplies of food and drink in Paradise. We are told how Allah provides believers with 'any kind of fruit and meat that they desire.' There will be banana trees 'with fruits piled one above another.' Bunches of fruit will 'hang low,' within easy reach. Supplies will 'never run out.'

The Koran also tells us that those good enough to qualify for eternal life will dine in style. 'They will be served by immortal boys,' it says. 'With cups, and jugs, and a glass from the flowing wine, wherefrom they will get neither any aching of the head, nor any intoxication. And fruit; that they may choose. And the flesh of fowls that they desire.'

This reference from the Koran that wine will be available in Paradise seems surprising at first glance. It is repeated elsewhere in the sacred text, with the righteous being told they will be offered 'rivers of wine delicious to those who drink.' On the surface, this commitment appears to conflict with yet another declaration in the Koran to the effect that intoxicants are 'an abomination,' with believers being warned to 'eschew such (abomination), that ye may prosper.'

The dilemma can be resolved by looking at both remarks in a slightly different way. Because the wine of Paradise is said not to cause 'intoxication' or 'aching of the head' it must therefore be non-alcoholic or at least not cause an alcoholic high. Problem solved, it seems! In that event, those selected to enter Paradise might be just as well off sticking to the water, which the Koran says will be pure, or the milk, which will never go sour!

It also seems that 'the fruit of the vine' will be available in the Christian heaven. We know, to begin with, that Jesus Christ consumed wine on earth. He is quoted, at one stage, as saying: 'The Son of Man came eating and drinking, and you say, "Here is a glutton and a drunkard."'

He is also quoted as saying, at the Last Supper, that he will drink wine again in paradise. Having raised the cup of wine, he gave thanks and the Apostles drank from it. He then said, 'I will not drink again from the fruit of the vine until that day when I drink it new in the kingdom of God.'

On the other hand, the early Church was wary of the effects of alcoholic drinks; so much so that it specified that those seeking high pastoral office should be 'not given to wine.' Perhaps, then, the consumption of celestial wine or any alcohol in heaven will be in moderation, although it seemingly will be available to those who wish to indulge.

Presuming that we do, indeed, meet near and distant family members, engage and spend time together, and share food and copious bottles of wine, the question arises as to how we will communicate with each other having forfeited our earthly capacity for speech. If the Bible is to be interpreted correctly, we may have a brand new language – the language of 'tongues'.

Although the Bible never specifically mentions a different heavenly language, Paul refers in Corinthians to 'the tongues of men and of angels.' To understand what he was alluding to by 'tongues' we must look to a strange occurrence mentioned in the Acts of the Apostles. It concerns an event that took place around Pentecost, in Jerusalem, where 'God-fearing Jews from every nation under heaven' were collected together and were touched by 'tongues of fire.'

Suddenly, although those who were speaking were Galileans, everyone could comprehend what was being said. 'Each one heard their own language being spoken,' the text informs us. 'Utterly amazed, they asked: "Aren't all these who are speaking Galileans? Then how is it that each of us hears them in our native language?"'

Listing where the people had come from – Rome, Egypt, regions of Libya, Asia, Judea, Mesopotamia, and many other places – they wondered how 'we hear them declaring the wonders of God in our own tongues.' Amazed and perplexed, they asked one another, 'What does this mean?' Some made fun of them and said, 'They have had too much wine.'

Although, as we have seen, there are major attractions to what we do in heaven, the cartoon we began with might still seem reasonably accurate in its depiction of the limited activities involved in passing an eternity there. Apart from the excitement of meeting former family and friends, along with the thrill of meeting angels and saints, there will be no marriage, little work except for singers and musicians, and we might all end up just sitting around eating, drinking and chatting in 'tongues'!

There are, however, two final heavenly occupations that just might fill our time. The first one involves taking care of what the astronomer and astrophysicist Carl Sagan once described as 'all that is, or ever was, or ever will be' – the Cosmos. This is mentioned in a reference in Genesis outlining Adam's duties at the time of the Creation. The relevant passage explains how God took Adam and 'put him in the Garden of Eden to work it and take care of it.' His job was to look after everything God had made, primarily the plants and the animals.

A piece of forbidden fruit and an unfortunate decision made by Eve put paid to that, resulting in 'painful toil' – a reference to the earthly hard work that would now be required of man. It was, from then on, about surviving through 'the sweat of your brow.' Not until the final judgement – and 'the new earth' – will things revert, with work as we now know it becoming redundant and our new job presumably being to care for the kingdom of God.

Two thousand years ago this kingdom of God was perceived in narrower terms than today. Although much less was known of distant land masses, far-off oceans or the magnitude of the wonders that hung in the sky, taking care of God's creation was still an onerous job. Add in today's cutting-edge knowledge of the planets, stars and galaxies – of supernovas, dark energy and dark matter – and the heavenly job of managing creation becomes a lot more exacting and demanding, to say the least.

The second, and final, heavenly occupation involves worshipping God, singing praise to the Lord, and simply revelling in the happiness and joy of being in his company. This is not a fanciful proposition; instead, it is a feature of the afterlife that is extensively chronicled both in biblical texts and in stories recounted by those who have returned from temporary death.

The Bible is full of references to the heavenly elect offering praise to God. The Book of Revelation – one of the central texts of the New Testament – describes the scene well. Revelation 19:6 puts it succinctly: 'Then I heard what sounded like a great multitude, like the roar of rushing waters and like loud peals of thunder, shouting: "Hallelujah! For our Lord God Almighty reigns."'

Revelation 7:9-10 further describes the joyous scenes: 'After this I looked, and there before me was a great multitude that no one could count, from every nation, tribe, people and language, standing before the throne and before the Lamb. They were wearing white robes and were holding palm branches in their hands. And they cried out in a loud voice: "Salvation belongs to our God, who sits on the throne, and to the Lamb."'

A similar scene, involving singing, instrument playing and offering adoration to God, was outlined in the late nineteenth century by Rebecca Ruter Springer, who we encountered earlier on in this book. Writing in 1898, in her book *Intra Muros*, she recalled arriving in the presence of God during her near-death experience. On seeing God, a vast concourse of souls burst into song as with one voice.

'Such a grand chorus of voices, such unity, such harmony, such volume, was never heard on earth,' she recalled. 'It rose, it swelled, it seemed to fill not only the great auditorium, but heaven itself. And still, above it all, we heard the voices of the angel choir, no longer breathing the soft, sweet melody, but bursting forth into paeans of triumphant praise.

'A flood of glory seemed to fill the place, and looking upward we beheld the great dome ablaze with golden light, and the angelic forms of the no longer invisible choir in its midst, with their heavenly harps and viols, and their faces only less radiant than that of Him in whose praise they sang.'

This sort of powerful, intense expression of joy and love associated with being in God's presence has also been articulated by many people I interviewed who had near-death experiences. Having seen, sensed or believed they were in the presence of God, they felt compelled to remain and revel in the sensation of joy. Nothing else mattered other than to stay where they were – warm, happy, comfortable and secure in the company of what they knew to be a kind and compassionate superior being.

It wasn't just their encounters with God that were blissful; *all* their encounters were positive, ecstatic and joyful. Nothing on earth could ever match the images and sensations they saw or felt. Everything was uplifting, including their meetings with deceased family and friends. They had clearly arrived in some sort of place or state containing all they had ever wished for

– a reward for the lives they had previously led, as we will see in the final chapter.

It is in that context that we should evaluate some of the wondrous features of heaven as described by our forebears over two millennia ago. To them, the struggle for food was more of an issue than today; having it in plentiful and lavish supply in heaven would have been a great blessing. In a world where the pleasures of life were limited, what could be more pleasing in heaven than the sweet sound of music? What they were really articulating in their heavenly descriptions was the sheer delight they hoped to experience after they died.

Perhaps, with that as a backdrop, the last words at this stage should go to Anne, who provides a modern-day expression of the joys of heaven. 'I'm not a religious person, but I remember phrases from the past like "lifting your soul",' she reflected. 'That's the only way I could describe it; it was like my soul being lifted. It was like mental, emotional, physical love all wrapped up in one. I didn't want to leave. I'd have loved to have stayed longer and I felt very sad coming back. But that's what happened. I was told to come back and I did.

'The feeling has never left me and I often think back to it. I don't have a fear of death now. When someone close dies, I feel differently about it. I don't grieve for them, even though I am sad and cry. I now feel they are gone home and I almost feel jealous of them. I think the place they go to is so beautiful and the feeling is so amazing. I think that's the result of what I went through.'

CHILDREN AND HEAVEN

A captivating painting titled *Christ Blessing the Little Children* hangs in the main stairway of the Walker Art Gallery in Liverpool. The canvas was commissioned in 1837 from the English artist Benjamin Robert Haydon. Known for the grand scale of his compositions, Haydon was dogged by misfortune – much of it financial – throughout his life, resulting in his death by suicide in 1846.

Haydon's painting is remarkable for two reasons. First, the artist was virtually blind when the work was commissioned, prompting him to regard himself as 'the first blind man who ever successfully painted pictures.' Second, and more important, the work depicts one of the most memorable scenes in the Bible where Christ extols the virtues of childlike innocence and promises children a place in heaven.

The scene will be known to anyone even vaguely familiar with the Bible, with both Matthew and Luke describing what had taken place. Having travelled 'into the region of Judea and across the Jordan,' Jesus was greeted by crowds who came to see him. Many brought along their little children so that he might place his hands upon them. The disciples rebuked them. Seeing this, Jesus was indignant.

He admonished the disciples: 'Let the little children come to me, and do not hinder them, for the kingdom of God belongs to such as these.' He then went on to explain the virtues of childhood: 'Truly, I tell you, anyone who will not receive the kingdom of God like a little child will never enter it.' Having finished, he took the children in his arms, placed his hands on them and blessed them. Such wonderful imagery was like manna from heaven, some 18 centuries later, for the artist Benjamin Robert Haydon.

This biblical narrative offers warmth and comfort to parents whose sons or daughters have died early in childhood or during adolescence. It brings solace to those who have lost a stillborn baby or a baby who died through cot death or from any other cause. Given their innocence – and the obvious love that Jesus had for children – the parents can reasonably expect that their deceased infant or child has gone straight to heaven.

The story also highlights the supreme value placed by Jesus on the many qualities of children, including honesty, innocence, openness to others, a desire to know the truth and, above all, humility and faith. It wasn't for nothing that he selected these characteristics as templates for the behaviour appropriate to a good life on earth and eventual entry to heaven.

By implication, we can expect to meet again our children in the afterlife. They, more than anyone, will be present in what Jesus called 'the kingdom of God.' Whatever that 'kingdom' might be – which we will be examining towards the end of this book – afterlife reunions will take place. Irrespective of how the children died – through stillbirth, cot deaths or other causes, or whether they were young or old – we will meet them again.

Stories featuring meetings with deceased children in heaven are regularly recounted by people who return from temporary death. Vivid encounters with dead brothers, sisters, sons and daughters, who died in tragic accidents or from various illnesses, are commonly reported. Reunions with babies who were lost through stillbirth or other causes of child mortality are likewise recorded in the literature.

One woman, Bernie, who mysteriously collapsed in 2007, described how she met with her deceased son Alan during her experience. He had died in 1981 in a tragic accident when a refuse truck reversed over him. He was aged five-and-a-half at the time. Although he had suffered extensive physical injuries in the accident, he looked perfect when she met him.

'His head had been crushed under the bin lorry but he had no scars, no bandages, nothing,' Bernie recalled. 'There was like a star behind his head. It wasn't like a halo. It was like in the shape of icicles coming out of his head. It was glowing so bright. There was also like a big light beyond him. I could see it way in the distance.

'He was right beside me, just the way he was at five-and-a-half. The only difference was this big glow around him. He said nothing. His hands were down straight by his side. There was nobody with him. It was so peaceful. He was on his own. He just smiled as if to say, "Mam, I'm OK."

'I was delighted he was there. I thought, "I'm going to see him! I'm going to him! This is it! This is it!" After he passed away I lived to die so that I could be with him. I was oblivious to everything else. Now I was going to Alan. But he wasn't reaching out to me. A neighbour who is older than I am later said to me, "When he hadn't got his hands out, he wasn't reaching for you. It wasn't your time to go." He then just disappeared.'

Biblical insights and information from other sacred texts suggest that Bernie might justifiably have been certain that she saw her dead son in heaven. These documents emphasise the preferential status given to children by God. Indeed, it should be noted that Christianity, according to the canonical gospels of Matthew and Luke, finds its very roots in the story of an infant birth in Bethlehem and not in any adult setting.

The New Testament contains interesting stories illustrating the affection Jesus had for children. Many of these narratives involve miracles and cures carried out at the request of the children's parents. The Gospel of Mark describes how a father brought his son to Jesus in the hope of securing a cure for the illness that had 'robbed him of speech,' caused him to fall on the ground, foam at the mouth, gnash his teeth and become rigid. He was cured.

The Gospel of Luke describes how Jesus raised from the dead the daughter of a synagogue leader. When he arrived at the father's house, he declared to those who were wailing and mourning: 'She is not dead but asleep.' Although they 'laughed at him,' he took her by the hand and 'at once she stood up.' We are also told how he drove a demon from a young girl and cured the dying son of a royal official at Capernaum.

Perhaps the most famous childhood biblical story involves the Old Testament ruler, King David. A powerful character, fearless in battle and believed to have authored a large part of the Book of Psalms, he governed Israel and Judah around 1,000 years before Christ. Jesus was one of his descendants, according to Matthew and Luke. At one stage, he incurred the wrath of God. The outcome was the death of his son.

The death of the child was the end result of an adulterous relationship King David had with the wife of a soldier in his army. After she became pregnant, he ordered the soldier to return from the field of battle hoping this might lead people to believe that he had fathered the child. When the soldier refused, King David ensured that he would be killed in combat.

The Book of Samuel tells us that the Lord was so unhappy that he swore revenge on the king, with one of the punishments being the death of his newly-born son. The child became ill. The king was understandably upset and repentant. He fasted and wept, and he slept all night on the ground. Unfortunately, on the seventh day, the child died.

A distraught King David expressed the belief that he would eventually meet his deceased son in heaven. 'I will go to him, but he will not return to me,' he said, inferring that they would be reunited one day in paradise, although until then they would remain apart. Eventually, King David and Bathsheba, the deceased soldier's wife, produced another son, named Solomon. 'And the Lord loved him,' we are told.

Perhaps King David was correct in his belief that he would meet his young child again, especially in the light of modern-day evidence from those who temporarily die. Many testimonies exist where people who had near-death experiences – and who beforehand had experienced miscarriage, stillbirth or infant death – met with their offspring in the afterlife. Discovering that their babies were secure and protected brought great relief.

Antoinette lost her baby in childbirth in 1971. After being released from hospital, she returned home and haemorrhaged twice. Rushed back into hospital, she haemorrhaged again and temporarily died. Having entered a tunnel and experienced the light, she found herself outside a beautiful garden, lush and green. Inside the garden, close to a bridge, was her baby, safe and secure, being guarded and kept from harm.

'I could see two figures on the far side of the bridge,' she recollected. 'One was an adult who was dressed in a white robe. He had long hair. I thought, at the time, that it was my father-in-law who had died just before that. I wasn't sure whether it was him or Our Lord. There was a baby lying on his shoulder. The baby was lying into him. I took it that this was the baby who died. I felt the baby was being minded, being protected.

'All I wanted to do was just get into the garden. It wasn't particularly that I wanted to get to the two figures. I just wanted to get to this place. I desperately wanted to be there. There was such peace in there. I thought, "If I can get to that place, and if it's going to be like that, it's going to be lovely, it's going to be rosy." I felt it was such a lovely place to be.

'I was nearly there, but I became conscious and woke up. They were calling my name and shouting and putting blood into me, there were tubes hanging out of my arms. I thought, "Oh, no! I didn't get there! I'm back here!" I was totally disappointed. Yet I now know I will meet up with my baby again. I have no doubt about that. The prospect of dying hasn't worried me since.'

In cases such as this – where the baby is lost early in childbirth – the question of whether it can enter heaven or paradise has caused controversy in Christian religions, especially Roman Catholicism, where the tradition – indeed, the obligation – of infant baptism has been practised since at least the second century.

The decision to ratify baptism as an obligatory procedure stemmed from remarks attributed to Jesus in the Gospel of John: 'Truly, truly, I say to you, unless one is born of water and the Spirit, he cannot enter into the Kingdom of God.' Without ritual cleansing – which may or may not be possible at the time of an infant's death or may be overlooked – the fear is that the child will be prevented from entering paradise and will instead be condemned to a lesser, more remote and less satisfying realm, often referred to as Limbo.

It must be emphasised, straight away, that Limbo, contrary to what is often believed, is not an official doctrine of the Catholic Church; nor has it ever been. It is not even mentioned or referred to in the Bible. Instead, it is a concept that was invented to solve a theological dilemma – namely, what happens to infants who die without having personally sinned but who are not baptised? This thorny issue has caused considerable Church conflict and debate, not to mention distress among parents of unbaptised deceased infants, for the best part of 2,000 years.

The problem facing the earliest Church theologians arose because infants, just like the rest of mankind, were believed to be blemished by original sin. Since baptism is necessary for the remission of original sin, therefore their souls cannot ascend to heaven. At the same time, not having personally sinned, how can they be condemned to suffer punishment in hell? Instead, it was concluded, they must enter an intermediate state after death.

The fourth-century philosopher, theologian and Archbishop of Constantinople, St. Gregory of Nazianzus, espoused this view. He outlined the position very clearly, stating that unbaptised infants 'will neither be admitted by the just judge to the glory of heaven nor condemned to suffer punishment since....they are not wicked.' He proposed, therefore, a neutral state where infants go and where they are free from punishment.

A pessimistic and damning counterview was outlined by St. Augustine, writing around the same time. Because unbaptised infants share in original sin, he claimed, they equally share in the appropriate sanction – in short, they are punished in hell for eternity. Augustine made one concession: that the punishment would be of the mildest kind.

For the next 1,600 years, a variation of both propositions – those of St. Gregory and St. Augustine – underpinned Catholic belief. The exact location of this abode of unbaptised but innocent souls became known as Limbo, meaning 'edge' or 'border', reflecting the view that this was somewhere adjacent to either heaven or hell, depending on your view.

Over time, some encouraging refinements were made to the concept, especially that Limbo might not be quite as grim as previously thought. Pope Innocent, for example, proposed that children who died and who were blemished solely by original sin suffered 'no other pain, whether from material fire or from the worm of conscience, except the pain of being deprived forever of the vision of God.'

St. Thomas Aquinas, writing in the thirteenth century, was even more affirming, proposing that Limbo was a location of positive happiness. The joy of those confined there, he said, would not be diminished or undermined by an understanding that their happiness would have been even greater had they been baptised.

At no stage, however, did the Church formally adopt any doctrinal position. Nor did they ever declare the non-existence of Limbo, stressing instead the importance of baptism and, as regards children who have died in an unbaptised state, entrusting them 'to the mercy of God.' Although they have recently proposed that 'there are theological and liturgical reasons to hope that infants who die without baptism may be saved,' they still regard Limbo as 'a possible theological hypothesis.'

The concept of Limbo for children is non-existent in Islam for the simple reason that the religion doesn't recognise original sin. Believing instead that Adam and Eve were both forgiven, it therefore follows that infants come into this world in a state of innocence. There is no intermediate state should they die before reaching puberty; instead, they go straight to Paradise where 'their souls are blessed' under the care of Abraham.

Protestants also don't believe in Limbo, arguing instead that deceased unbaptised infants go straight to God. Presbyterians, in particular, reject the concept, believing that infants who die before they become accountable are saved. Mormons take a broader view, claiming that people who die with no knowledge of the gospel – who would otherwise have embraced it – become 'heirs of the celestial kingdom of God.'

It might reasonably be argued that the concept of Limbo – confined, as it has been, to the speculation of Catholic Church theologians – is sufficiently outmoded and unfounded in biblical terms to warrant its dismissal by concerned parents who have lost an unbaptised child. 'The kingdom of God belongs to such as these,' ought to be recalled as the ultimate view of Jesus on children, as we have seen at the top of this chapter.

It is also common for people who have near-death experiences to meet young brothers and sisters who had died a long time ago and who, as a result, are difficult to recognise. Many of these children may have been lost in childbirth or when young and are therefore hard to identify when encountered at the borders of heaven. Occasionally, they may have died before their siblings were born.

The following story is a case in point. It involves a man named Paddy, who left his body in the course of a heart bypass and valve-replacement operation. During his experience he was greeted by a brother he had never even known, who had passed away when young from meningitis. In this instance, although Paddy had never met the brother before, he was able to establish quickly who he was. The event occurred in 2009.

'I saw my brother John, who had died a long time ago, at the age of ten,' Paddy recalled. 'I remember my mother telling me that they had brought him to hospital and she had spent days and nights holding his head to keep the pain away. One night he was in terrible pain and he died the following morning. There was no cure at that time for meningitis.

'I never knew him because I was born after him and I had never seen him. He was the oldest child in our family. I had only seen him in pictures and he was a fine fellow. I know my parents were very upset by his death. My father was buried not long after; he was heartbroken and he got cancer. My mother had to bring the rest of us up and it was no fun at that time. She eventually died at the age of 76.

'John and my mother and father were together when I saw them. My father-in-law was there, too, exactly the same as when I knew him. There were lots of other people, but I couldn't recognise most of them. My parents were sitting in a sitting-room with their backs to a wall. There was a table in front of them. My brother was sitting between them. He looked older than he was when he died; he looked maybe 17 or 18 or in his 20s.

'I could see all of them clearly. I could recognise John because he was the image of my son. I recognised him, as well, from photographs. Also, once I saw my mother and father, I could put it together and I knew it was him. They were all looking at me and they were happy. He was happy-looking, too. I had the idea that he wanted to talk to me, but I wasn't there long enough for that to happen.

'I know they were in heaven when I saw them. My brother was in heaven because he had died so young. He had harmed nobody. My mother and father were good people, too. I was happy to know they were there.

'I believe, when I die, they will all come to meet me again, including my brother. I wonder what he will say to me. I'm sure he will ask me what I have been doing. I will be very happy to see him and I am certain we will meet again.'

As we saw in the chapter discussing the people we meet in heaven, those who reside there are said to look well. Bodily imperfections have disappeared, injuries have healed, blemishes caused by the ravages of illnesses such as cancer have faded away. Sometimes, aspects of personal appearance, such as hair-style, seem to be different. General demeanour, however, is one of happiness, leaving new arrivals well-pleased.

One woman, named Mary, described meeting her younger sister, who had died in a fire. Despite having been physically damaged, she looked normal and well. None of the effects of being in the fire were evident. Although she was immediately recognisable, there was one big difference – her hair seemed unfamiliar. She was also bathed in light.

'It was bright and I could see my sister clearly,' Mary said. 'She was about the same age as the last time I had seen her, about 12. She was life-sized. But she wasn't in normal clothes and her hair was different. Everything was white – her clothes and her face – but her hair was black.

'She was wearing like a white, flowing dress and her hair was shorter. I wondered why her hair was shorter because she had lovely long hair when she was alive. There was kind of a light around her. It wasn't a bright light, more like a glow or an aura. She didn't seem scared. She was just Patricia, my sister. When something happens like what happened to me you think, "There's got to be something." And I definitely believe there is something else there.'

Tony saw his 21-year-old son, who had died in a car accident. In this example, once again, there were some slight, unexpected changes in his physical appearance. Although he was instantly recognisable, and his mood was good, the hairstyle he sported when alive had changed. He was also, like many other reported cases, bathed in light.

'He was dressed in normal clothes but there seemed to be a glow around him,' according to Tony. 'It was a yellowish glow. He was lit up and in wonderful humour. When he was alive he would have tinted his hair a bit but that was all gone and he was very normal-looking. His hair had gone back to its original colour. Immediately after speaking to me, he was gone. As a result, I believe Anthony is in heaven. And I believe that one day I will meet him and be reunited with him again. I just can't wait.'

Up to now we have heard from adults describing images of heaven and the children they met there, which were witnessed either as visions or while in the throes of temporary death. There is, however, another side to this phenomenon – namely, where young children themselves experience temporary death and return with extraordinary descriptions of what they saw. These experiences can occur at any age. Given their forthrightness and honesty, children's accounts are widely regarded as being highly credible.

The eminent psychiatrist and pioneer of near-death studies, Dr. Elisabeth Kübler-Ross, researched this territory from the 1960s up to her death in 2004, producing excellent studies and books along the way. She also documented many remarkable stories, including one involving a young girl who woke up one morning with an extraordinary tale to tell.

The girl described how, during the night, she had met Jesus, who informed her that she was going to die and enter heaven. Although normally a quiet, reserved child, she was filled with euphoria at the prospect of what lay ahead. She described the silver and gold, the rubies and precious stones that were there. She spoke of how she would take care of her mother from afar. That afternoon she was dead, murdered by intentional drowning.

Another prominent near-death researcher, Dr. Melvin Morse, undertook a major study of childhood case histories, resulting in the publication of his bestselling book *Closer to the Light*. In it he featured many stories of childhood temporary deaths including the example of a young boy who, at the age of three, told his parents about what had happened to him when he was only nine months old.

Having suffered a cardiopulmonary arrest at that young age – which he hadn't ever been told about – he described how he had left his body, met his deceased grandparents, entered a tunnel and headed for a distant light. He also described how he had come to a bright place where he ran through fields with God. God asked him if he wanted to return home. Although he didn't wish to do so, he was told he could come back again another day. He then returned to his body.

A further example chronicled by Melvin Morse involved an eight-year-old girl who almost drowned after her hair got caught up in a swimming-pool drain. Having blacked out, she floated from her body and headed through a tunnel towards a distant light. She eventually arrived in what she understood to be heaven. In fact, she *knew* it was heaven because brightness was everywhere and everyone was so happy. She then met a kind man who asked her if she wanted to stay. Having considered his offer, she told him she wanted to return to her family. This she did.

In my own research, I too encountered many case histories where young people reported visits to the other side. Among those I spoke to was a 14-year-old who left his body having almost drowned. Not only did he travel through a tunnel to a distant light, but he also encountered strange figures and experienced a comprehensive life review.

With no more air in his lungs and aware that death was seconds away, he suddenly felt a hand on his back pushing him up. 'It wasn't a closed hand; instead, it was fully open and I could feel the fingers,' he recollected. 'It was in the centre of my back. As a result, I came up out of the water. When I came to the top, I was about three feet away from the edge and the hand pushed me in to the side.

'I would love somebody to tell me what that hand was. People say it was the hand of God or my guardian angel, but I don't believe in guardian angels. I also didn't think at the time about whose hand it was, but I do think about it now and I am definitely sure it was a hand. That hand is on my back all my life.'

In a number of my previous books I examined the additional phenomenon of deathbed visions. These occur when people who are fading away report seeing dead family members arriving from the afterlife and welcoming them to the other side. Usually, these are familiar people who were once known and loved, such as parents, spouses, children or friends. Less often, people report seeing angels or other religious figures. These visions are experienced by children to the same extent as adults.

Deathbed visions have a profound impact on those who are passing away. They normally bring great serenity, contentment, peace of mind and a 'good death'. Apprehensions and distress disappear. Pain eases and is replaced by perfect calmness. The dispirited reveal a sense of elation. They are heartened, reassured and happy. These positive effects are felt by children, too, and are widely reported.

The following story, concerning one of these heavenly visits, was related to me by a woman named Philomena, whose young daughter Patricia had drowned tragically in 1968. Many years later, when her husband was dying following a heart attack, it was evident that their deceased daughter came to visit him. This is how Philomena described the scene.

'He had been downstairs for a cup of coffee and then we got him back up to bed,' she remembered. 'After a few minutes he said to me, "Who is the lovely girl by my bed?" It was about 11 o'clock in the day. At this stage, I didn't know how lucid he was so I pretended it was our other daughter Dolores. But he said, "Not at all, Phil. Dolores has gone downstairs long ago. Who is this beautiful blondie girl?" Dolores is dark but Patricia was fair.

'He only said it once. At that, his face lit up. He knew who it was. He never mentioned her name. He never spoke to her. All he did was follow her around the room, with a smile on his face. That's all he did, all that time, was watch her. You knew that she was moving because he was following every move.

'The expression on his face said it all. It gave me such comfort. He kept asking me, "Phil, say another one of your prayers." And he kept following her around the room. That went on until he died, that same evening, with me beside him holding his hand.'

The arrival of long-lost young family members also features in the following story described to me by a man named Tony. He outlined who his mother met shortly before her death in 2002. Each of the people she mentioned had already passed away. She saw deceased parents and siblings, but she also saw a brother who had died at a young age and a sister who had died as a baby.

'The next thing, my mother said, "Look! There's Mum!"' Tony recalled. 'After that, she called out her father. She then called out each of her brothers. She also called out her sister. She then put her hand up to her face in surprise and she said, "Oh! It's Brí!" I was puzzled by this, as I had never heard of a Brí before.

'I just turned around to my eldest sister and I asked her, "Who's Brí?" She said to me, "Don't you know?" She then went on to explain, "That was a sister you had who died about a month after she was born." I think I would have been around six or seven at the time.

'My mother continued, "Jimmy, it's me, Mary!" I later discovered that Jimmy was only about eight years of age when he died. We said afterwards that my mother had got older since then, so she was introducing herself to him. She finished by saying, "I'll see you all shortly!"

87

'She was smiling as she said the names. She was happy and staring into the distance, down to the bottom of the bed. She was clearly delighted to see her family. It was as if she hadn't had a stroke. The following day, she gave a deep sigh, squeezed my hand and she was gone.'

Case histories documenting similar deathbed visions involving young children were also compiled in Victorian times. Some of them described long-lost young brothers or sisters coming to those who were dying; others recalled young children being visited by older deceased family members or other unknown figures.

Many of these stories were chronicled by the distinguished physicist Sir William Barrett, who for many years was Professor of Experimental Physics at the Royal College of Science in Dublin. Author of many books, including *Death-bed Visions* and *Psychical Research*, he was knighted in 1912.

One of the many examples recorded by Barrett in *Death-bed Visions* concerned the last days of a boy whose older brother and sister had passed away some time before. The little boy, who succumbed to illness at the age of four, described how his two deceased siblings had come to visit him shortly before he died.

He said to his father, 'There's Fred and Annie.' 'Where?' his father asked. 'Don't you see them there?' the boy responded, pointing towards the wall, 'they're waiting for me to go to them.' A minute later the boy fell back dead on his pillow. It is worth noting that the father witnessed nothing of the two deceased children, although he believed his youngest child's version of events.

A second example profiled the remarkable experience of a perfectly healthy three-year-old who said she had been visited by her recently-deceased aunt. One day, her mother asked her why she was looking fixedly out the window. 'It is Aunt Louise, who holds out her arms to me and calls me,' the child replied. Although her mother attempted to distract her, she continued to stare through the window for several minutes.

Some months later, the child contracted tubercular meningitis and was confined to bed. One day she claimed that her aunt had once again come to visit her and was calling her while surrounded by angels. 'She is holding out her arms to me,' the child told her mother, who was reduced to tears. 'Don't cry,' the young girl said, 'it is very beautiful, there are angels round me.' She died shortly afterwards, four-and-a-half months after the death of her aunt.

A further story recalled the death from tuberculosis of a 14-year-old boy, who wasted away rapidly over a period of four or five months. About a week before he died he called his mother to tell her that he could see a door at the corner of his room. 'When it is open wide I shall be going through it,' he said.

On the day he died, he called his mother once again. She found him sitting up in bed, staring at the corner of the room. 'There is a nice old man come for me,' he said, 'he is holding out his arms for me. I must go.' He then fell slowly back in his bed and died with a smile of joy on his face.

To end this chapter, it is instructive to return once more to where we began – to the Bible and the great love shown by Jesus to children. Although explicit biblical pronouncements about children and heaven are not plentiful, when they are present they are powerful. When directly involving Jesus, they represent some of the most forceful images to be found in these ancient texts.

Matching the evocative scene where Christ blesses the little children – so well captured by the British artist Benjamin Robert Haydon, mentioned earlier – there is another incident involving the disciples and children. This scene is set towards the end of the Messiah's long walk through Galilee, where he met with ordinary people while preaching, converting and performing miracles. Conducting this trek on foot, he was followed by his disciples, who were clearly impressed and excited by the popular response to their leader.

Believing that Jesus was going to set up an earthly kingdom, the disciples wanted to know who among them would be appointed to the most powerful and prestigious posts. The Gospel of Mark tells us that they had been discussing this as they walked along. They were, however, too embarrassed to question him about his intentions.

Suspecting that something was afoot, when they arrived at Capernaum – a thriving fishing village which Jesus used as a headquarters for his public ministry – he asked them: 'What were you discussing on the way?' Initially, they held their peace and said nothing. Deducing what the issue was, Jesus sat the 12 disciples down and told them bluntly: 'If anyone wants to be first, he shall be last of all and servant of all.'

He then took a child and 'set him before them,' the Gospel of Matthew informs us. Lifting the child in his arms, he said to his disciples: 'Truly I say to you, unless you are converted and become like children, you will not enter the kingdom of heaven. Whoever then humbles himself as this child, he is the greatest in the kingdom of heaven.

'And whoever receives one such child in my name receives me; but whoever causes one of these little ones who believe in me to stumble, it would be better for him to have a heavy mill-stone hung around his neck, and to be drowned in the depth of the sea.'

He continued by voicing the much-quoted parable of the faithful shepherd. Of the shepherd's 100 sheep, he said, even if only one of them strays he will set out to find it, and he rejoices over it more than the 99 that have not strayed away. Pointing at the child in his arms, he concluded: 'In the same way, it is not the will of your Father in heaven that one of these little ones should be lost.' There could be no more clear-cut commitment to a child's right of entry to heaven than in that simple statement uttered by Jesus that day.

DO ANIMALS GO TO HEAVEN?

A most interesting story is told regarding the journey to heaven of the legendary Indian king Yudhisthira. The tale is recounted in an epic poem which is believed to have been composed up to four centuries before Christ. Its central character – the king – is a man of great honour and righteousness. The other main character is his loyal dog.

While travelling to his final resting place, involving a long trek over mountains, Yudhisthira was accompanied by members of his family and his faithful dog. One by one the family members died. As a result, only Yudhisthira and the dog arrived at the gates of heaven. 'You may enter,' the king was told, 'but your dog may not.'

Yudhisthira was greatly distraught. Conscious of the animal's loyalty and devotion, he refused, opting instead for an afterlife in hell or a return to earth. Immediately he was informed: 'It was only a test, now you may enter.' He had shown himself to be morally righteous by being faithful to his dog.

According to the epic poem *Mahabharata*, the dog was immediately transformed into the great deity Dharma, who praised Yudhisthira for his virtues. Yudhisthira then entered heaven. Modern versions often end the tale with both king and dog entering paradise. Either way, this colourful narrative has survived down through the ages and has been replicated in numerous written forms and on TV.

The story of Yudhisthira's dog is a fruitful starting point for examining whether all God's creatures – including humans, pets, farm animals and wild beasts – achieve eternal life. The issue is highly controversial, involving many moral and religious complexities. As we have seen from the story above, the topic is not just a modern one; instead, it has arisen in the discussions and folklore of most cultures and creeds stretching back to earliest times.

From the early Egyptians and ancient Greeks to the Vikings, a fundamental belief was that animals live on in the hereafter. Although it is often assumed that these ancient civilizations and their religions were so preoccupied with humans that they had little interest in the afterlife of animals, the reality was entirely different.

The Egyptians mummified dogs and buried them with their masters, believing they would accompany them to the other-world. A most interesting example concerns the high priestess Maatkare whose preserved body was discovered with a small bundle lying at her feet. Initially believed to be her child – which caused surprise as high priestesses were meant to be celibate – it turned out when X-rayed to be her pet monkey.

Cats also figured in ancient Egyptian beliefs, where they were accorded sacred status. Many cats – not just those belonging to royalty – were mummified. The same care would be given to preserving a cat as preserving a human. They would then be buried alongside containers of milk and mummified mice as sustenance for their travel to the hereafter.

Because of these burial customs, many of the names used by early Egyptians for animals have been preserved over time. Some dogs' names were heroic, such as Brave One and Reliable; others were descriptive, such as The Black, Ebony and Town

Dog; more were based on their characteristics, such as The Grabber, Cook Pot and Useless. Many dogs' names were also built around the half-word 'abu', which was most likely the Egyptian version of 'bow-wow'. All these well-loved creatures were presumed to accompany their masters to paradise.

Seven thousand miles from Egypt, many Native American tribes had a similar understanding of the afterlife. Their other-world was believed to be a replica of the physical world, only much happier and with an abundant supply of animal life. Some far-north tribes spoke of the presence of caribou, seals and salmon; others spoke of beavers, porcupines and moose.

Another indigenous tribe, the Saponi, originally from the southern state of Virginia, believed that afterlife animals would be copious and fat. With so many animals present, it wasn't for nothing that several tribes, especially those from the Great Plains, referred to the land of the dead as 'the happy hunting-ground'.

Back in Europe, the ancient Greeks, like many other believers in reincarnation, maintained that both animals and humans had immortal souls which were reincarnated from one to the other. They also believed that a vicious dog – multi-headed and named Cerberus – guarded the entrance to the underworld, stopping the living from entering and the dead from leaving. He was the ultimate 'Hound from Hell'!

At its core, the issue of whether animals live on after death depends on whether you believe, or don't believe, that man is supreme and holds dominion over what some people regard as the lower animal world. Philosophers, theologians, scholars and ancient wise men – not to mention pet lovers – have addressed the issue for over two millennia, producing a mass of confusing, contradictory and sometimes misleading conclusions.

Perhaps the most widely held view is that animals either don't have souls or, if they do, their souls are not immortal, thereby precluding them from everlasting life in the company of God. Only man has an immortal soul, this argument goes. If you accept this argument, the inference is clear – animals, as inferior beings, are not present in paradise.

This viewpoint first originated with the earliest Christian theologians and moral philosophers who linked the soul to man's ability to reason. Man, being rational, they argued, is superior to animals and therefore the only species capable of eternal life. It is the capacity to think that determines the right of entry to paradise: man possesses it in spades; unfortunately, animals do not.

Prominent Church thinkers – principally St. Augustine and St. Thomas Aquinas – were to the forefront in perpetuating this view. Augustine referred to 'brute animals' lacking a divinely-sparked human intellect and therefore being denied life after death. Aquinas agreed, arguing that because animals lacked intellect they were therefore 'not made in God's image.' Since only those made 'in God's image' could escape death, it was good news for mankind while animals were ruled out of the picture.

Glaringly obvious flaws were always apparent in this dogmatic afterlife philosophy. In particular, it was based on the notion that all animal actions are derived from mere instinct and never from the power of thought. This denial of an animal's ability to reason and think must have been clearly contradicted by the evidence available at the time.

Just like today, it must have been obvious that elephants had sophisticated memories, chimpanzees were adept at problem solving, and various other creatures – including crows – possessed the ability to figure out complex issues in their struggle to find food. It must have also crossed people's minds that if someone as young as a baby or a child qualifies for an afterlife, then so also should a creature with manifestly more advanced reasoning skills, even if that intellectual imbalance lasts only for a limited period of time.

The 'rationality' argument had the additional side effect of condemning animals to the role of servants of man, useful for work, as a source of food and as objects for cruelty. Aquinas put the case succinctly: 'We refute the error of those who claim that it is a sin for man to kill brute animals. For animals are ordered to man's use in the natural course of things....Consequently, man uses them without any injustice, either by killing them or by employing them in any other way.'

This argument additionally led to a rejection of the idea that animals possess emotions even though, once again, it must have been obvious that they, just like humans, felt pleasure and pain, experienced terror and fear, and could be joyful and sad. It would have been readily apparent that they became stressed and anxious. Acute grief would have been expressed by many, especially baboons and elephants. Some, most notably dogs, would have revealed themselves to be capable of intense loyalty, warmth and affection.

While theologians and moral philosophers were dismissing animals and their souls, early populations, including the first Christians, took a polar opposite view. They had a profound respect for animal life and shaped their practices and beliefs accordingly. So intense was their belief in the value of 'God's creatures', and their role in God's plan, that many eschewed killing animals and restricted themselves solely to vegetarian diets.

The initial followers of Christ, known as Ebionites, refrained from eating animal flesh and banned animal sacrifice, having most likely learned this philosophy directly from Jesus. Another prominent religion, Manichaeism, which was founded in the third century and spread widely, also espoused vegetarianism, especially the eating of green and yellow foods. St. Augustine was a follower of Manichaeism for a decade.

Respect for animals was also evident among individuals. St. Clement of Alexandria, writing at the end of the second century, described how Matthew – one of the Twelve Apostles – survived on 'seeds, nuts, and vegetables, and no meat.' Another work, dating from the early third century, explained how the Apostle Thomas – who many believe to have been the brother of Jesus – lived on 'bread with salt, and his drink is water.' A further third-century text outlined how the Apostle Peter survived on bread, olives and vegetable soup. All three, in other words, were vegetarians and rejected the exploitation of animals.

Other well known figures of the time avoided eating animal flesh. The mathematician and philosopher Pythagoras, who lived some five to six centuries before Christ, believed in the immortality of the soul and survived without eating meat. Numerous church luminaries followed suit in later centuries, among them saints such as Clare, Kevin, Benedict, David, Dominic, Jerome, Joseph of Cupertino and Catherine of Siena.

St. Francis of Assisi also adopted a compassionate attitude towards animals and believed they were not to be subjugated, mistreated or exploited. He articulated his viewpoint with simple clarity: 'All creatures have the same source as we have. Like us, they derive the life of thought, love and will from the Creator. Not to hurt our humble brethren is our first duty to them; but to stop there is a complete misapprehension of the intentions of Providence. We have a higher mission. God wishes that we should succour them whenever they require it.'

There are numerous stories of St. Francis's affinity with the animal kingdom – how he was followed everywhere by a lamb, his sermons to the birds, his taming of a wild wolf, how his donkey cried at his deathbed after the saint thanked him for carrying him during his life. Not surprisingly, he believed they, too, possessed souls. 'Does every creature have a soul?' he asked. 'Surely they do, for everything God has touched will have life forever. And all creatures he has held.'

While popular opinion and compassionate saints veered one way, the official view became even more entrenched. Efforts intensified to diminish animals and elevate their human counter-parts. In the process of doing so, some serious liberties were taken. To understand them we need to revisit the original biblical texts, which were initially written in Hebrew, Aramaic and Greek and only later translated into Latin and numerous other languages. What we find is quite shocking.

In the process of translating from one language to another, and over the passage of time, various key biblical teachings were misinterpreted and distorted in an effort to elevate humans above the animal kingdom and single them out for everlasting reward. The end result was a man-made fabrication where original references to the immortal souls of animals were lost, resulting in their exclusion from eternal life.

At the centre of this deception was the translation of two simple Hebrew words, 'nephesh' and 'chayah', with a favourable interpretation being attributed to humans, a much less favourable one to animals. The true meaning of the words is straightforward: 'nephesh' refers to 'soul'; 'chayah' refers to 'living'. Put them together and the result is 'living soul'.

Let us now turn to Genesis, where the origins and nature of humans and other creatures are described. Regarding humans, the text tells us that 'the Lord God formed man of dust from the ground and breathed into his nostrils the breath of life. And man became a nephesh chayah.' In other words, man became a 'living soul', with all the attendant prospects for immortality that such a description implies.

Regarding animals, the original Genesis text is equally clear: 'God created the great sea monsters and every nephesh chayah that moves.' Genesis likewise tells us that the Lord brought all the wild animals and all the birds in the sky to Adam 'and whatever the man called a nephesh chayah, that was its name.' In other words, animals, too, were 'living souls'.

Over time, however, the preponderance of authoritative Bible translations rendered 'nephesh chayah' as 'living soul' when referring to man and to 'living creature' when referring to animals. 'Living soul' is almost never attributed to both, in contravention of what was intended in the original text. 'Tragically, our English Bibles hide this fundamental truth by translating nephesh one way when it refers to animals and another when it refers to humans,' concludes Norm Phelps when assessing this topic in his study *The Dominion of Love: Animal Rights According to the Bible.*

From a purely religious perspective, it was also suggested that, whatever the beliefs might be of individual saints and disciples, the great sacred texts had nothing to say about the role of animals in the afterlife. Even today, it is often argued that these texts, notably the four canonical Gospels, state clearly that animals lack an immortal soul and therefore cannot enter paradise. Both assertions couldn't be further from the truth. Not only do the most revered sacred manuscripts stress that animals are as much God's creatures as man, but they also tell us that they too survive death.

The Old and New Testaments mention numerous species of animals, including dogs, wolves, camels, deer, bears and lions, together with insects and other creatures. These textual references help us understand not only the many animal species that were present at the time of Christ, and the uses they were put to, but also their role in the divine scheme of things.

Perhaps the most compelling religious depictions of animals are associated with events surrounding the birth and death of Jesus Christ. It is traditionally accepted – although at no time mentioned in the four Gospels – that an ox and donkey were present at the nativity in Bethlehem. Camels associated with the Magi, and sheep associated with the shepherds, were later additions to the scene.

There is textual evidence to support at least some elements of this conventional nativity representation. 'Between two animals you are made manifest,' the prophet Habakkuk predicted six centuries before Christ, hinting at the presence of the ox and donkey. Subsequent religious writings, including the Gospel of Pseudo-Matthew in the seventh century, stated that they were there.

An animal is also acknowledged in the lead-up to the Last Supper and the Crucifixion, when Jesus is described in all four Gospels as entering Jerusalem on the back of a donkey. We are told how he instructed two disciples to go to a nearby village and borrow a donkey that would be standing there, promising its later return. With disciples' cloaks draped on its back, Jesus then entered Jerusalem on this humble symbol of kindness and peace.

The Gospels also emphasise the intrinsic value of animals. In Luke we read how Jesus stressed to his disciples the worth of even the smallest of God's creatures: 'Are not five sparrows sold for two pennies? Yet not one of them is forgotten by God.' In Job we are informed how animals can teach us spiritual lessons: 'Ask the beasts, and they will teach you; and the birds of the air, and they will tell you....and the fish of the sea will explain to you.'

We learn in Numbers how the prophet Balaam was rebuked by an angel for beating his donkey three times. 'Why have you struck your donkey these three times?' the angel demanded to know, while stressing that Balaam's actions were 'perverse.' In Genesis we are told how God instructed Noah to save from the flood 'pairs of every kind of bird, and every kind of animal, and every kind of small animal that scurries along the ground.'

Given these and many other references, it is no surprise to discover that animals turn up in paradise. In the Book of Revelation, for example, we are given a graphic description of heaven and the countless features to be found there. It is an extravagant work, wonderfully written in the first century by a person named 'John' who, as mentioned in a previous chapter, is most likely to have been John the Apostle.

Revelation provides a dramatic and picturesque description of the throne of God, which is surrounded not only by 'ten thousand times ten thousand' angels but by elders and 'four living creatures.' These creatures have pride of place encircling the throne. One is described as being like a lion, another like an ox, a third like an eagle and the fourth with a face like a man.

These animals, we are told, bow before God and offer praise to the Lord. 'Whenever the living creatures give glory, honour and thanks to him who sits on the throne and who lives for ever and ever, the twenty-four elders fall down before him,' we are informed. Not only does this description constitute a clear reference to the presence of animals in heaven, but it attributes a central role to them at the feet of God.

Revelation also provides us with an apocalyptic account of the fall and destruction of Babylon. Following vivid descriptions of the city's moral decay and the avarice of its merchants, we read how heaven opened to reveal 'a white horse' on which the 'King of Kings and Lord of Lords' sat. We are also told how the Lord's armies, dressed in fine linen, white and pure, followed him 'on white horses.' Once again, the presence of animals in heaven is highlighted.

Further evidence regarding the afterlife of animals can be unearthed in the Book of Ecclesiastes, which is part of the Old Testament and Hebrew Bible. The relevant comment is worth examining with care: 'What happens to the children of man and what happens to the beasts is the same; as one dies, so dies the other. They all have the same breath, and man has no advantage over the beasts, for all is vanity. All go to one place.'

The meaning of that statement is crystal clear: there is no difference between man and animals. Both possess the same 'breath' – the biblical word used to denote 'spirit' – and both end up in the same destination, in other words in paradise. Just as man doesn't return to nothingness, nor does his animal counterpart. Their ultimate destiny, on death, is the same.

It is worth pausing here to emphasise that many near-death experiences confirm the picture outlined so far – namely, that animals appear prominently in paradise. A number of eminent researchers in the field have reported noteworthy and convincing cases. Most of them involve former pets; other ones involve animals of no known connection with the person who has died.

Some of the animals emerge to greet adults who have temporarily died; others step forward to welcome children. Their purpose, it often seems, is to act as guides. Mostly smaller animals, such as dogs or cats, are involved. Great scenes of happiness and excitement are recalled. Descriptions frequently include scenes where tails are wagged, people are licked or nosed, and both animal and human are overjoyed to be united once again.

A brief but interesting example dates back to 1898 and the lady we heard from earlier in this book, Rebecca Ruter Springer. Having arrived in paradise following temporary death, she met one of her former dogs, an intelligent and faithful animal named Sport. She spotted him among a group of children who were playing with him, rolling and tumbling in the grass.

'As we approached he broke away from them and came bounding to meet us,' Springer recollected. Former owner and animal were delighted to meet up with each other, with Rebecca stooping, placing her arms around his neck and resting her head in his hair. The dog, she said, 'responded to my caresses with every expression of delight.'

A further example, dating to 1951, concerns the experience of a man facing imminent death. The story was related by the man to his daughter and eventually featured in the book *The Truth in the Light* by Dr. Peter Fenwick and Elizabeth Fenwick.

Not only did the man see the light and feel intensely happy, but he also encountered all the dogs of his life including one from his early boyhood years. They were running towards him, excitedly jumping about and wagging their tails. It was clear they were coming to him to welcome him. Instead of going to them, however, he was told it wasn't his time and to go back. This he did. He passed away soon afterwards.

A similar narrative was chronicled by the well-known near-death researcher P.M.H. Atwater in her book *Beyond the Light*. The story was recalled by a man who had been hospitalised following an acute allergic reaction to a food he had eaten. Not only did he experience tunnel travel and approach a bright light, but he was also greeted by former pet dogs.

The first dog he met was a poodle he had once owned, which raced towards him, jumped in his arms and licked his face. Everything about the dog was authentic, including his smell, his breathing, and the great joy he exhibited at being with his former owner. He later saw other former pet dogs, which also arrived on the scene.

Throughout all this, the man experienced a life review and a meeting with deceased relatives who appeared to be both healthy and happy. Although he wanted to stay, he wasn't permitted. Instead, he returned through the tunnel and arrived back in the hospital, where he was told that he had died for more than ten minutes.

Hospice chaplain and author Dr. William Serdahely added a further remarkable story to the literature, involving the near-death experience of a seven-year-old boy named Pat. The boy almost drowned when he fell from a bridge while fishing with a friend. Not only did he travel through a dark tunnel, but he also met two of his former pets. The pets, a cat and a dog, had died four years earlier.

The case history bolstered Serdahely's research conclusion that in the case of the death of a child whose parents and siblings are still alive, it is often former pets who come to meet them. Likewise, the process of sending them back is often initiated by these animals, as evidenced in the story of Pat whose dog sent him back to the physical world.

Jan Price further described meeting a former pet while on her travels following a near-fatal heart attack. Having entered the light, where she felt wonderfully at peace, she was greeted by her once much-loved pet dog Maggi. The dog – a Springer Spaniel – was as real to see and touch as she had been in the physical world. She had died less than a month before and had been sorely missed.

Together they travelled through a realm of ecstatic colour, playing and having fun. Jan was able to stroke the dog again, while the animal laid her paws across her former owner's legs. They eventually reached a wonderful realm full of beautiful gardens containing flowers, fruits and plants arranged in perfect patterns.

The dog led Jan to a 'temple of knowledge' and a joyful city full of harmony and light. There she was shown a kaleidoscopic representation of her life. After experiencing true joy, oneness with God and a profound understanding of all that is, she returned to her body. As she explained in her book *The Other Side of Death*, the last image she returned with was of her dog Maggi's face.

It is worth noting that communications with animals have also been reported by many mediums, who claim to have heard or seen a wide range of former pets, including cats, dogs, birds and horses. Cases have been reported where the descriptions provided are accurate according to the mediums' clients; on occasions, correct names of the pets have also been identified. These experiences add to the picture of animal survival after death.

Animals have also featured in my research stretching back over many years. Of the hundreds of people I have interviewed – on issues concerning temporary death, deathbed visions and other related themes – various creatures, especially pets, have turned up in their accounts.

It was inevitable, following the publication of these stories, that I would be contacted by people concerned regarding the afterlives of their animals or with further narratives to relate. Some people wanted an answer to the question: 'Will I meet my dead pet in heaven after I die?' Others described strange events surrounding the deaths of their cats or dogs. The following is the experience of one person I spoke to, Edel, who believed that the soul of Pixie, her cat, which had been killed in a road accident, came to her to say goodbye.

'One day I was on my way home from work,' Edel recalled. 'I stopped a short distance from home and did some shopping. Afterwards, I got back in the car. I was driving away when my car filled with Pixie's smell. It was a very distinctive smell. It felt like she was in the car, to the point that I wondered should I pull over to see if she was in the boot.

'Eventually, the smell left the car and I was approaching the house where we live. It is located at the bottom of a hill. When I got to the bottom, who was there only Pixie! She had been knocked over and was dead on the side of the road. I was in an awful state and phoned my husband. He said, "I only left the house a very short time ago and I fed the two cats at the back of the house. She was alive when I left." So I had got the smell around the same time that Pixie was killed.

'I believe Pixie had come to me to say goodbye. I had a definite sense of that. I thought she had come to say she was moving on. That evening, I was going into town with my husband and he asked me, "Do you get Pixie's smell in the car?" I couldn't get it then, but he got it. To me, that was really significant. He was really fond of the cat. I think Pixie had come to him, too.

'I believe everything has a spark of life. The fact that we, as humans, believe that we have that spark more than animals puts them in a very subordinate position. Instead, I think that we all share the same air and we all have souls, including Pixie, and I also don't think any of us goes from this to nothingness.

'I don't know if where we all end up will be in the form we currently know on this planet. I think it will be more like the Hindu concept that we're all a spark and we all gel in together as part of the Brahman, the bigger reality. So I don't know that when I pass on I'll see Pixie in a cat form, but we'll all be part of the one, whatever that "one" is.'

That Edel turned to Hinduism to explain her perception of the afterlife is significant as it, too, just like Christianity, is a religion with much to say about the otherworld prospects of animals. Not only do Hindus understand animals to be manifestations of God, but they also believe they possess souls and are subject to the same cycles of birth and death as humans.

Animals are colourfully represented in Hindu religious art and temple architecture. They also appear in depictions of gods – for example, the god Ganesh has the head of an elephant. So important is the status accorded to animals, and so valuable their perceived contribution to everyday life through work and self-sacrifice, it is no surprise to discover that Hindus form the greatest percentage of world vegetarians.

A similar respect for animals exists in Buddhism, which is founded on the belief that all creatures are reborn after death and that the process of death and rebirth is repeated over time. A person may be reborn in any form – animal or human – and the procedure takes place over and over again until nirvana is achieved.

The result is that all creatures form part of an interconnected web. Any dog, cat, bird or fish may have once been your relative or best friend. A wild or domestic animal might once have been your grandfather, mother or son. With this process stretching back over time, it can be said that all humanity and all forms of animal life are linked.

Buddhists, as a result, show the same kindness and compassion to animals as they would to a mother, brother or sister. Animals are afforded utmost respect. They should not be made to suffer. Hunting is cruel and, therefore, wrong. Vegetarianism is widely practised because, after all, the killing of an animal is like the killing of one of your kin; the eating of an animal is like consuming a relative or friend.

It is equally instructive to look to Islam, where we read of birds and animals in Paradise although what species are there is 'known only to Allah.' It is also stressed in the Koran – Islam's sacred text – that animals and humans share common features. 'All the creatures on earth, and all the birds that fly with wings, are communities like you,' we are informed. More pertinently, the text adds that animals, like humans, 'shall be gathered to their Lord in the end.'

A most interesting Islamic hadith – or 'prophetic tradition' – tells us about the importance attributed to dogs. The story describes how a man was out walking and became thirsty. Spotting a well, he climbed in and drank until his thirst was quenched. As he emerged, he saw a dog panting and licking moist mud, clearly dehydrated. 'This dog has become as thirsty as I was,' he said.

He climbed back into the well and filled his shoe with water. Clutching it between his teeth, he then climbed back up again and quenched the thirst of the dog. According to Muhammad, Allah thanked him for his actions and forgave him his sins.

Another story from Islam concerns cats. It involves the Egyptian author and grammarian, Ibn Babshad, who lived in the eleventh century. One day, he and some companions, while eating on the roof of the mosque in Cairo, spotted a cat and gave it some meat. Taking the meat in its mouth, it departed only to return for more a short time later. This it did over and over again.

Knowing that the cat couldn't have eaten all the meat on its own, he and his friends decided to follow it. The cat climbed over a wall on the roof and down into an empty space. There they found another cat, but blind, who was eating the food which was brought to it.

Overwhelmed by what he had witnessed – and believing it to be proof that God makes provision for all his creatures – Ibn Babshad sold his property, renounced his salary and lived in poverty until his death in 1077.

A third and final story further illustrates the respect Islam affords animals. This story concerns the Prophet Muhammad and his love for his favourite cat, Muezza. One morning, on hearing the call to prayer, this founding father of Islam arose from his bed to discover Muezza asleep on the sleeve of one of his robes. Not wishing to disturb the cat, he cut off the sleeve, dressed and headed to prayer, leaving Muezza in peace. Legend has it that, on his return, the cat having woken bowed to Muhammad, who patted her three times on the head.

Tradition likewise has it that Muhammad, who is believed by Muslims to be the 'messenger of God', had an affection for cats so great that he gave the nickname Abu Hurairah, which translates literally as 'father of the kitten', to one of his closest companions who was also a cat lover. On a broader note, he was so concerned about animals that he commanded that they should be treated with kindness and respect.

It is stories such as these, along with the content of sacred texts, the witness reports of those who die temporarily and the traditional beliefs of multiple societies dating back to the very beginning of recorded time, that establish an overwhelming case for the survival of animals after death. Should Christians have any doubts about this, they might recall that the Bible clearly states that 'all things are possible with God.' Should that mean God satisfying a soul's desire by allowing for the company of former animal friends then so be it!

This point is further emphasised in Islam, especially in the Prophet Muhammad's teachings. 'There will be everything you wish to have and you feel like seeing,' the Prophet promised regarding the hereafter. 'All that the souls could desire, all that their eyes could delight in' will be there. Even if you wish to 'wander on the back of a horse made of red rubies, it will fly you wherever you want.' Can there be anything more emphatic than that?

Modern evidence from the world of quantum mechanics has substantiated these assertions and beliefs. As you will see in the final chapter, there is every reason to believe that all animate and inanimate things survive physical death and live on in the hereafter. Nothing can decline into nothingness; there is no disappearance of consciousness whether animate or inanimate. So whatever your particular pet might have been – a dog, cat, horse, donkey or any other species of animal – you will meet them again in what is often referred to as 'heaven' or 'paradise'.

REINCARNATION

Two weeks before Christmas 1926, a baby girl was born in Delhi, India. Her name was Shanti Devi. There was nothing remarkable about this middle-class child during the early years of her life. At the age of four, however, things changed. She began to speak of her former husband and son, describe her husband's shop, the food she ate, the clothes she wore, the life she led. Although mystified, her parents decided to ignore her.

Her former name, she said, was Lugdi. Years later, when she was nine, she disclosed her husband's name as Kedar Nath Chaubey, a shopkeeper who lived in the city of Mathura near Delhi. Upon investigation, it transpired that he had indeed lost his wife, Lugdi, who had died giving birth to the couple's son.

What followed had all the ingredients of an epic detective story. Letters were exchanged and details of Shanti's recollections confirmed as correct. Next, a meeting with a cousin of the husband was arranged. Shanti immediately recognised him and identified who he was. He interviewed her and concluded that the girl was his relation personating in another body.

The husband also came to visit. He was introduced as his brother, to see if Shanti might be misled. She immediately spotted the deception, saying that he was not her husband's brother but the husband himself. His physical features were exactly as she had previously described them. The foods she asked her mother to cook were his favourites. Every recollection tallied, including confidential details which she shared with him in a private discussion. He was convinced that she was, indeed, his former wife.

News of this remarkable girl soon spread through Delhi, then India, followed by the world. Intrigued by the case, Mahatma Gandhi spoke to Shanti and instigated a commission of inquiry. They accompanied her to Mathura, where she recognised family members, identified locations, recalled many obscure details and answered all relevant questions accurately. The commission concluded that the case was a genuine example of reincarnation.

The story of Shanti Devi came to prominence in a country with religious beliefs rooted in the principle of reincarnation. Given that the vast bulk of the population – some 80 per cent – are Hindu, her experience reflects the predominant religious philosophy. It is a philosophy based largely on the notion of cyclical death and rebirth.

What lies behind the belief is simply described in the ancient Bhagavad Gita: 'Just as a man discards worn out clothes and puts on new clothes, the soul discards worn out bodies and wears new ones.' This basic principle underscores not just Hinduism but other Indian religions including Sikhism and Jainism. It likewise appears in Eastern faiths such as Taoism.

Belief in reincarnation was also prominent in early forms of Christianity. This is evident from many sources, among them a most extraordinary text known as the Pistis Sophia. The document, which was written at an unknown time but probably in the early centuries following the death of Jesus, was discovered in Egypt in the eighteenth century.

The Pistis Sophia not only describes the general teachings of Jesus to his disciples, but it specifically states that he espoused the doctrine of rebirth as a universal law governing the lives of mankind. It also declares that the prophet John the Baptist, who is said to have baptised Jesus, was the reincarnation of the earlier prophet Elias. It goes on to outline how souls repeatedly return to earthly life until they have unravelled the mysteries of light and expunged the guilt connected with their sins.

Early support for reincarnation also found expression in the writings of some of Christianity's first theologians. One of the most prominent in the third century was the prolific scholar and author Origen Adamantius. Unfortunately for Origen, the Church, which was formulating a centralised, unified, coherent philosophy at the time, was opposed to his views. They didn't sit well with the 'one soul, one life, one judgement' direction the Church was taking. He was condemned, with his theories concerning reincarnation described as heresies.

Spurred on by Origen's alleged heresies, the Church sprang into action. The doctrine of rebirth was denounced by various religious bodies and councils. The Council of Constantinople, in 553, put its case unequivocally: 'Whoever shall support the mythical doctrine of the pre-existence of the soul and the consequent wonderful opinion of its return, let him be anathema.' The die was cast, the decision made, the case closed, there was no turning back – reincarnation, as far as Christianity was concerned, was dead and gone as an issue.

The Council of Constantinople's statement in 553 had far-reaching repercussions for the subsequent direction of religious belief in Western society. Not only was a chasm opened with the religions of the East but by the medieval era in Europe only alchemists and mystical philosophers were left to believe in reincarnation – and they had to do so in secret to avoid persecution. With the later spread of Christian missionaries across America, native tribes eventually lost their beliefs, too, with the exception of those in isolated areas in the northwest.

The face of Celtic Europe was changed, also. The early Celts had been ardent believers in reincarnation. This was noted by Julius Caesar, who worried that his Celtic adversaries didn't fear death because they believed that 'souls do not die, but pass from one body to another.' This, he was aware, was bad news for his troops.

The Greek historian and philosopher Alexander Polyhistor, writing around the same time, described how the Celts accepted that their souls would 'enter into another body.' The noted Roman poet Marcus Annaeus Lucanus – whose name is often abbreviated to the more manageable 'Lucan' – also referred to this proposition in his first-century epic poem *Pharsalia*. Celtic warriors, he remarked, believed it was only a coward who would 'grudge a life sure of its return.'

Dr. Douglas Hyde, scholar and first President of Ireland, was able to conclude in his *Literary History of Ireland* how 'the idea of re-birth which forms part of half a dozen existing Irish sagas, was perfectly familiar to the Irish Gael.' This was no longer so following the spread of Christianity through Europe, with its tentacles reaching to the far outposts of Ireland. It was like a form of religious cleansing, with the landscape of many Western societies changed, as a result.

The belief that the soul, upon bodily death, returns to earth in another body or form originated in the earliest philosophies of India. Exactly when and where the belief first emerged is unknown. The concept was vaguely mentioned in the ancient Indian texts known as the Vedas, dating as far back as 1700 BC. It was also briefly referred to in scriptures written around 700 BC. Although it must have been evolving by that time, it didn't achieve common acceptance until three centuries before Christ.

The Hindu understanding of reincarnation has an engaging simplicity at its core. At the time of physical death, only the body disintegrates. The soul, on the other hand, travels away and enters another body. This process is repeated over and over until the soul achieves perfection. Only then can the soul unite with the Supreme Soul or God.

How the soul achieves perfection is down to karma. Karma is all about action and carrying out good works and virtuous deeds. Good actions and good deeds result in good karma; when our actions and deeds are bad the result is the exact opposite. You carry your karma with you, from one body to the other, from one life to the next. How we acted in the past determines what we are today; how we act today determines our future.

There is no guarantee that we will return as humans. It is possible, instead, that we might return as an animal or a lower form of life. It all depends on the amount of karma we have accumulated. If we have stored up good deeds and behaved well, we may return in human or super-human form. If we have stored up bad or evil deeds, we are likely to reincarnate in a lesser form. The ultimate goal is to escape this cycle and achieve salvation.

This concept of repeated incarnations is well understood and accepted by followers of Hinduism. It is represented first and foremost in beliefs concerning Vishnu, one of the religion's three principal Gods, who is the great lord of preservation, sustaining the universe and ensuring that its laws are upheld. It is said that he has incarnated on earth in various guises.

There are ten forms Vishnu is usually understood to have taken or will take in the future. He first arrived on earth as a fish, then a tortoise, a boar, a strange half-man and half-animal, a dwarf, warrior, king, the deity Krishna, Buddha and, finally, he has yet to appear as Kalki who will come to destroy evil and restore moral order. In all these incarnations, his purpose is to vanquish negative forces of evil and to display his divinity.

Similar beliefs in reincarnation have featured in Indian life down through the ages. Examples are plentiful. They include the widely-believed reincarnation of a poet who lived before Christ into the form of another poet born in the sixteenth century. It was predicted that the original poet, Valmiki – who wrote one of the great Indian epics, the *Ramayana* – would reincarnate at a future stage. This he did, it is said, in the form of the Hindu poet Tulsidas, who composed a retelling of the *Ramayana*.

Modern-day Indian reincarnations are also widely reported. A recent example concerns a boy born in the early 1980s by the name of Toran 'Titu' Singh. From an early age, he spoke to his mother about his 'children' and 'wife', his educated sisters-in-law, the car he once owned, that he came from a wealthy family in Agra where he had a shop in 'Sadar Bazaar,' and that he wanted to 'go home.'

He referred to his brother and sister by name and identified his shop as 'Suresh Radio,' which sold transistor radios. His eldest brother did some research and located a shop called Suresh Radio in Sadar Bazaar in Agra. He also discovered that the owner of the shop – Suresh Verme – had been shot dead around the time when Toran was born.

Suresh's family came to visit the boy. He instantly recognised Suresh's father and mother and two brothers. He described his former family home, including lamps it contained and a room 'which remains locked.' He also gave a vivid description of how he had been shot – by three people, near his house, but he didn't see their faces. He stated that they had approached him from the left side and then ran away. All these details were accurate.

On being brought to Agra, an attempt was made to trick him by bringing him to a different shop. He instantly knew he was being deceived. Later, he identified the correct shop, noted changes that had been made, singled out the cash drawer from a number of identical drawers, and identified the shop manager by name.

American researcher Dr. Antonia Mills travelled to India to investigate this strange case. Among the details she recalled in her subsequent study was how Suresh's family, at their meeting with Toran, noted that the boy had a birthmark similar to a bullet entry wound in the same part of the head where Suresh had been shot. They also noted small birthmarks at the rear of his skull where the bullet might have exited. These details were confirmed by Mills.

Dr. Mills concluded that in Toran's case – as in other cases she studied – she found no evidence of fraud or fantasy, and stressed that they were part of the growing body of cases for which normal explanations did not do justice to the data. The data, she said, although not offering incontrovertible proof of reincarnation 'offer evidence of the survival of some element of the human personality after death.'

Just as the near-death experience enables us to know what happens when the soul travels to either heaven or hell, it would be interesting and instructive to find out what occurs when a soul is reincarnated. Are the patterns similar? Is there departure from the body, tunnel travel, a bright distant light, arrival at a border or boundary, encounters with deceased family or friends, judgement, and a meeting with the superior being? Is there a sense of peace? How is the rebirth accomplished? It would be most useful to gain insight to the process involved.

As it happens, it wasn't Toran 'Titu' Singh but the person mentioned at the top of this chapter – Shanti Devi – who provided precisely those insights. In a sequence of interviews, and on one occasion under hypnosis, she outlined what happened when she died as Lugdi, the wife of Kedar Nath Chaubey. The following is a summary of what she said.

Not only did she experience a 'profound darkness' – probably tunnel travel – but she also saw a 'dazzling light.' 'Then and there I knew I had come out of my body in a vaporous form and that I was moving upwards,' she said. She was then met by 'four men in saffron robes,' with all four in their teens and their appearance and dress 'very bright.'

She came to a river, or border, into which 'those who aspired for a higher life sincerely, but who had committed fleshly wrong in this life, were dipped' before moving higher. She then came to the 'huge' and 'dazzling' throne of Lord Krishna, one of the great Hindu deities.

There she was shown a record of all her activities on earth, good and bad, and advised as to what would happen to her in the future. The god examining her record was Chitragupta, who we will read more about in The Book of Life chapter. She was then led to 'a place like a staircase,' which was bathed in light. Finally, she was taken to a 'dark room' and was made to lie down in a clean part of it. This 'dark room' was most likely the womb from which she would later emerge into her next life.

Remarkably, considering the subcontinent she originated from and her religious background, the stages she outlined were almost an exact replica of those commonly described in the near-death experience of Western culture. All the elements were there, and similar emotions felt, with the notable exception of the 'dark room' or womb which facilitated her return to a new life.

The concept of rebirth is also a basic tenet of Buddhism. Like Hinduism, Buddhism proposes that physical death is not an end and supports the idea of continuity into the future. Although the basic principle is similar, there is one distinct difference. Buddhism rejects the idea of a permanent 'self' or 'soul' that passes from one body to the next. Instead, we are part of an evolving consciousness. At death, what occurs is a bit like the flame of a dying candle lighting the flame of a new one. In this way we are reborn.

This doesn't stop Buddhists from describing their past lives. A representative example, which occurred in Japan in the early nineteenth century, was chronicled by the noted author Lafcadio Hearn. Hearn had been born in Greece in 1850 to an Irish father and a Greek mother. Having eventually moved to Japan, he became one of the country's most popular authors, with works including the book *Gleanings in Buddha-Fields*.

In the book, Hearn recounts the story of a young boy named Katsugoro who, at the age of nine, told his sister about his previous existence and subsequent rebirth. His father, Kyubei, was a farmer, he said. He identified the village he came from and explained how he had died at the age of six from smallpox. He also explained how, when he was five years old, his father Kyubei had died and was replaced in the family home by another man named Hanshiro.

The boy provided a detailed account of his death, outlining how he had been placed in a 'jar', as was the custom in Japan at the time. 'I was buried on a hill,' he recalled. 'There was a hole made in the ground; and the people let the jar drop into that hole.' He clearly remembered the sound of the jar dropping into the hole. He then described his afterlife journey.

A very old man, who looked like his grandfather, took him away. 'As I walked I went through empty air as if flying,' he recollected. 'I remember it was neither night nor day as we went: it was always like sunset-time. I did not feel either warm or cold

119

or hungry. We went very far, I think; but still I could hear always, faintly, the voices of people talking at home; and the sound of the Nembutsu (a Buddhist chant) being said for me.'

He also remembered the food offerings being made for him after he had died, and could particularly recall inhaling their vapours. He then described how the old man eventually guided him to his current home. 'We came here, and he pointed to this house, and said to me: "Now you must be reborn – for it is three years since you died. You are to be reborn in that house."'

Just like Shanti Devi, he was unclear about the exact details of his rebirth, although he said he was born 'without any pain at all.' This feature of being unable to fully recall the rebirth, it seems, is common in cases such as this.

Word of this remarkable story spread quickly. 'The boy repeated all the circumstances of his story with so much exactness and apparent certainty, that the Headman and the elders of the village made a formal investigation of the case,' Hearn wrote. It turned out that the details of the boy's recollections were true. Not only did the family exist, but their son Tozo had died of smallpox at the age of six. Other details also proved to be accurate.

In due course, Katsugoro was brought to his former village, where he immediately identified his previous home, noted accurately how a tree and tobacco shop were new, and convinced the family – especially his former mother – that he had, indeed, been her deceased son. She and her new husband 'caressed Katsugoro and wept,' we are told.

The writings of Lafcadio Hearn, which first arrived in the West in the late nineteenth century, opened up the culture and religions of Japan to a fascinated public in America and Europe. Japanese religious beliefs regarding reincarnation became widely known, as a result.

Similar developments occurred concerning India, where trade and, in particular, the work of the East India Company prised open the subcontinent to the gaze of the developed world. Knowledge of Indian customs and practices, including what were considered 'strange' beliefs about reincarnation, spread far and wide.

Simultaneously, fascination with affairs concerning the human 'spirit' or 'soul' came to the fore in the West. Séances were held, mediums became popular, and discussions and lectures about reincarnation and mankind's afterlife destinies were convened. Famous names including Arthur Conan Doyle, Charles Dickens and William Butler Yeats were hooked. Even Mary Todd Lincoln, following the death of her son, held séances in the White House which were attended by her husband President Lincoln.

Hypnosis and many Oriental practices including meditation also became popular in the nineteenth century. The use of hypnosis to assist recall of past lives was at first discussed, then trialled and, by the 1950s, perfected. Past-life regression became a popular technique for eliciting secrets hidden in a person's soul. Soon, extraordinary stories were emerging about people's past lives, causing interest in reincarnation to grow rapidly.

One of the most remarkable reincarnation stories from the twentieth century was recorded under hypnosis over a 10-month period from 1952 – 53. It involved a woman named Virginia Tighe, aged 29, who was interviewed while in a hypnotic state in Colorado, USA. After being put into a deep sleep, she revealed the intimate details of a previous existence in Ireland.

Her former name, she said, was Bridey Murphy and she had come from Cork. Her mother's name was Kathleen; her father's name Duncan. She had a brother, also named Duncan, and had another brother but he had died as a baby when she was four.

Her bedroom was upstairs in the family home – 'up the stairs and turn to the left,' she said. 'It's very nice.'

She described many scenes in her life – playing house with her brother, while aged eight, in 1806, and scratching the paint off her bed as a four year-old. 'It was a metal bed,' she explained. 'Dug my nails on every post and just ruined it.' She spoke of family holidays in Antrim, and described scenes featured on the journey from Cork to Belfast.

She showed a remarkable knowledge of many Gaelic words – frequently using the word 'lough' for 'lake' and mentioning the Uilleann pipes. She also revealed knowledge of Irish mythology, referring to Cuchulain, Deirdre of the Sorrows and to other events of a historical nature. She additionally stated that her father was a 'barrister' – using a word not commonly used in America – and that she was taught at school by a Mrs. Strayne.

She outlined how she married a man by the name of Brian MacCarthy, whose parents lived in Cork but who studied and lived in Belfast. He later taught at Queen's University and had appeared in the Belfast *News Letter*. She lived there with him, childless, until her death at the age of 66. She 'fell down the stairs,' she said, and 'broke some bones in my hip too, and I was a terrible burden.'

Bridey died on a Sunday, she recollected, when her husband was at church. 'It upset him terribly that he wasn't there,' she said. She then described – just like Shanti Devi did before her – what she experienced and saw after her death, including observing her husband, visiting her brother in Cork, meeting her deceased younger brother in the afterlife, and attending her funeral.

Like Shanti Devi and Katsugoro, however, she was unable to comprehensively describe her rebirth. When asked under hypnosis how she was reborn, she merely replied: 'I....left there and I was....born....and I lived in America again,' referring to her rebirth in 1923.

Subsequent investigations established the accuracy of much of Virginia Tighe's recollections. Descriptions of the landscape between Cork and Dublin proved to be accurate, Belfast shops she had identified by name had existed, and many other details were verified. Some of the details, however, proved impossible to establish and substantiating evidence could not be found.

Not surprisingly, this remarkable story eventually featured in a bestselling book, *The Search for Bridey Murphy*, by Morey Bernstein, the hypnotist who had conducted the regression, and it also became a movie of the same name. It inspired popular songs, including *The Love of Bridey Murphy*. The story remains to this day a controversial, yet significant, landmark in reincarnation research.

Stories such as Bridey Murphy's, as recollected by Virginia Tighe, are in no sense dissimilar to equivalent reincarnation accounts dating far back into history. Although it is a modern-day narrative, dating from the early 1950s, it could have been chronicled at any time in the last 3,000 – 4,000 years. It is also only one of many hundreds of credible reincarnation reports that have been compiled – and continue to be compiled – in recent times.

Things have come a long distance from the time when, in territories bar those in the East, the idea of reincarnation became so suppressed that it wasn't even afforded discussion. As the German philosopher Schopenhauer wrote in 1851: 'Were an Asiatic to ask me for a definition of Europe I should be forced to answer him: It is that part of the world completely dominated by the outrageous and incredible delusion that a man's birth is his beginning and that he is created out of nothing.'

Despite the conventional wisdom that has pertained since the Council of Constantinople stamped its agitated feet in 553, reincarnation has continued to attract followers ranging from philosophers to world statesmen, from pragmatic businessmen to creative artists, composers and authors. Old and much newer proponents include Leo Tolstoy, Napoleon, Mark Twain, Benjamin Franklin, Nietzsche and Voltaire. Others include Mahatma Gandhi, who believed that in some future birth he would see world peace.

Carl Jung, the esteemed Swiss psychiatrist, was yet another believer: 'My life often seemed to me like a story that has no beginning and no end. I had the feeling that I was an historical fragment, an excerpt for which the preceding and succeeding text was missing. I could well imagine that I might have lived in former centuries and there encountered questions I was not yet able to answer; that I had been born again because I had not fulfilled the task given to me.'

Henry Ford, the founder of the Ford Motor Company and the first to use mass assembly-line production techniques in manufacturing cars, was a believer, too. Puzzled by the nature and origin of genius, he came to the realisation at the age of 26 that it was the result of what was learned over many lives. 'Genius is experience,' he said. 'Some seem to think that it is a gift or talent, but it is the fruit of long experience in many lives. Some are older souls than others, and so they know more.'

Ford's moment of revelation put his mind at ease. 'When I discovered reincarnation it was as if I had found a universal plan,' he reflected. 'I realised that there was a chance to work out my ideas. Time was no longer limited. I was no longer a slave to the hands of the clock....The discovery of reincarnation put my mind at ease. I would like to communicate to others the calmness that the long view of life gives to us.'

Perhaps that last remark from Henry Ford pinpoints one of the most attractive features of reincarnation – that death is no longer an end in itself; instead, it is a new beginning. Therefore, what we ultimately achieve and contribute is the result of many lives and not just of one brief existence on earth in one bodily form.

Reincarnation has other appealing features, too – for example, it may explain why our personal misfortunes are not necessarily of our own making; instead, they may result from the actions of others before us. It also teaches the need to take responsibility for our future and for the future of others. It additionally offers us a second chance – the hope that if we do good deeds and undertake good actions, we can become better not just here but in our lives ahead.

Lastly, the notion of reincarnation forces us to pause for thought when contemplating the issue of survival after death. Reincarnation may mean that our consciousness continues to exist after death not in some independent form but as part of the consciousness of other beings, within whom it is reborn or reincarnated. Such a form of consciousness rebirth is a most interesting thought and not without support, but more of that in the final chapter.

THE BOOK OF LIFE

Believers in Hinduism encounter two gods when they die. The first is Yama, who is the god of death and ruler of the departed. He is waiting in his court, ready to judge them. Beside him sits another god, his assistant Chitragupta, who keeps records of people's good and bad deeds from birth to death. It is on the advice of the latter that afterlife destinies are decided.

Yama looks fearsome and has fiery eyes. He carries an iron rod in one hand and a noose in the other. Chitragupta has an entirely different disposition. He looks calm and serene, wears an ornate headdress and sports a neat, well-oiled moustache. He dresses in bright, colourful clothes and is depicted holding a scroll in his hand detailing the events of dead people's lives.

Chitragupta has a curious history. At one stage, Yama went to Brahma, the god of creation and one of the three great gods of Hinduism, complaining of the difficulties keeping proper records of men's actions in life. Unfortunately, it seems, he was sometimes so confused that he directed souls the wrong way. Brahma thought about it for 'thousands of years' until, one day, a man emerged from his body holding an inkpot and pen. The ultimate bookkeeper, or accountant, was born!

Since then, Chitragupta has logged the lives of mankind, detailing all their actions, good and bad. He watches over everyone, keeping track of everything they do. The end result is the most complete, impartial register of man's deeds. It is this register – and the nod from Chitragupta – that determines where souls are consigned after death.

This notion of a register of man's deeds which is stored at the gates of heaven and consulted at a person's death is one of the oldest and most powerful religious images ever devised. It generates fear, primarily because we know it will force us at death to face the reality of all our actions in life, good and bad, including our darkest deeds.

Everything we have done, to ourselves, to our families, to others, will be listed. Nothing will be missed, nothing concealed, in this record of our passage through life. Hidden secrets will be exposed, crimes revealed, wrongdoings uncovered, deceits unveiled, leaving us to confront the transparent and unedited balance sheet of our lives.

The chances of being unmasked during the assessment are high; the prospects of emerging unscathed are low. That the final judgement will end with being assigned to one of two entirely disparate destinations – a heaven full of happiness or a hell filled with horror – ensures that the process is all the more formidable.

There are many names for this record of life's deeds, each one connected to a specific religion. We have already encountered Chitragupta's register in Hinduism, but the concept is also prominent in Christianity where it is often referred to by the title of this chapter – the Book of Life. References to it can be found throughout scripture.

One of the Psalms informs us that those who are not righteous should be 'blotted out of the Book of Life.' Paul, in Philippians, asks for help for his fellow workers 'whose names are in the Book of Life.' The Book of Daniel explains how 'everyone who is found written in the book' will be rescued. Ominously, God declares in Exodus: 'Whoever has sinned against me, I will blot him out of my book.'

Perhaps the most powerful and dramatic evocation of the Book of Life is chronicled in Revelation. This apocalyptic document outlines John's vision of the Second Coming of Christ. Compiled in the first century, it provides a vivid description of how this register of life's deeds, along with other subsidiary texts, is used at the time of judgement.

'I saw a great white throne and him who was seated on it,' John wrote in Revelation. 'The earth and the heavens fled from his presence, and there was no place for them. And I saw the dead, great and small, standing before the throne, and books were opened. Another book was opened, which is the Book of Life.

'The dead were judged according to what they had done as recorded in the books. The sea gave up the dead that were in it, and death and Hades gave up the dead that were in them, and each person was judged according to what they had done. Then death and Hades were thrown into the lake of fire. The lake of fire is the second death. Anyone whose name was not found written in the Book of Life was thrown into the lake of fire.'

This notion of being assessed or judged after death is far from being a fanciful religious dogma or a curious feature of texts underpinning world faiths. Instead, it sprang into existence a long time ago, in a wide variety of landscapes, spanning many continents, cultures and creeds. Millennia later, it remains one of the most intriguing features of the near-death experience.

Those who die temporarily often recollect judgements where events from their past lives pass before their eyes. They normally refer to the phenomenon as a 'life review'. Although it frequently happens in the presence of what they know to be a 'superior being' or 'God', the being most often has no direct involvement in the process. Instead, the assessment is undertaken solely by the person who has died. To put it simply, you judge yourself.

Monica is a typical example of someone who went through a self-assessed life review. She did so in the late 1970s having haemorrhaged following a miscarriage. A young woman at the time, she was 'bleeding non-stop' and felt herself to be 'fading away.' Rushed to hospital, she was being wheeled down the corridor when she felt her 'mind, or soul, or spirit,' as she put it, rise above her body to a place of 'beautiful quietness.'

'Then I saw flashes of events from my life,' Monica told me. 'It was like some sort of a review starting with my teenage years. They were very happy times in my life. The best way I can describe it is that it was like flicking through a photo album and experiencing again all the thoughts and emotions I had experienced when the photos were taken. The photos were in black and white and were kind of over on my right-hand side.

'I saw one scene where I was out dancing, which I loved. I was jiving. I could feel the excitement inside me again. I saw myself when I was young going to school with my sister. There was nothing negative and there was nothing in my life I was ashamed of or guilty about. My life was being relived and I have to say I felt incredibly happy. I didn't want to come back.'

Many near-death interviewees also describe how they judge themselves through the eyes of others – in other words, through the eyes of those they have affected. This makes the judgement process infinitely more daunting. It is one thing to convince yourself that your behaviour towards others has been thoughtful and considerate; it is another thing entirely to assess your behaviour through their eyes. You might be shocked by what they think.

To familiarise ourselves with the most important ancient reference to afterlife judgement, we need to go back to the late 1800s and to Luxor in Egypt. It was there, in 1888, that E. A. Wallis Budge, an Egyptologist with the British Museum, came across one of the most important manuscripts in history. After hearing rumours of a major archaeological find, he travelled to Luxor and was astonished by what he discovered – 'the largest roll of papyrus I had ever seen, tied with a thick band of papyrus, and in a perfect state of preservation.'

The document was a copy of the Egyptian Book of the Dead written for an important temple scribe named Ani, who lived more than 1200 years before Christ. The purpose of the text was to provide everything a dead person needs to know to guide them through the underworld and into the afterlife. It could justifiably be claimed that its depiction of judgement is one of the most important images ever discovered.

A focal point of the judgement scene is the 'Balance' or the 'Scales of Justice'. We see Ani entering the judgement area, where his heart is weighed against a feather. The heart reflects what is good or bad about a person's life while the feather is a symbol of what is 'right'. If the heart doesn't balance with the feather, the person is condemned to non-existence and cast to a beast which devours him.

Luckily for Ani, the judgement went smoothly and the final outcome was favourable. 'His heart is righteous,' the manuscript informs us, 'and it hath come forth from the Balance; it hath not sinned against any god or any goddess. Thoth (an Egyptian god) hath weighed it according to the decree pronounced upon him by the Company of the Gods, and it is most true and righteous. Grant thou that cakes and ale may be given unto him, and let him appear in the presence of the god Osiris.'

While the outcome for Ani was positive, the same cannot be said for the priceless papyrus. Having been purchased by Wallis Budge for the British Museum, he proceeded to cut it into 37 distinct sheets for ease of handling, affecting the continuity of the document. Sometimes chapters were cut in mid-sentence; images were cut the same way, too. He also glued the sheets to wooden boards for display purposes, with the glue eventually causing damage. Judgement, I'm afraid, was probably not too kind on this employee of the British Museum!

In its purpose and effect, the scales of justice is a mirror image of the Book of Life. Both achieve the same end result – a comprehensive and impartial evaluation of a person's actions in life. All things of relevance – the treatment of others, the reckless chasing after selfish gain and the unsavoury and uncharitable behaviours – are laid bare. Nothing is excluded, nothing hidden away.

Anyone observing the still-standing entryway to Notre-Dame Cathedral in Paris will see an identical scales of justice to the one just described. Carved in stone over their heads is an 800-year-old depiction of the judgement facing humanity after death. All the great participants are there – the saved and the damned, angels and devils, intercessors and mediators, with the figure of Christ overshadowing them all.

The real focus of interest is the scales of justice. An angel is positioned on one side of it; a grotesque devil on the other. Which way it balances determines our fate. We either join the line of exalted souls looking happy and gazing upwards to God; or we join the line of downcast sinners being led off in chains to hell. No more than a few feet separate the two groups carved into the archway; the gap undoubtedly feels greater for those who have just died.

French royalty and presidents, great scientists and church statesmen, the rich, the poor and the famous have all passed beneath this famous judgement portal at Notre-Dame. It was there for Napoleon's crowning as Emperor, Mary Queen of Scots' marriage to the Dauphin of France, Henry VI's crowning as King, the funeral services of presidents including Charles de Gaulle, and visits by Pope John Paul II. It is doubtful if any of them could have missed the significance of the judgement scene carved into this great Gothic portal.

Similar scales of justice are reported in many vision accounts recorded down through the ages. The concept is particularly well described in the vision of Thurkill, a thirteenth-century Londoner who embarked on a voyage through the afterlife. Among the images he returned with was a clear description of a scale fixed in perfect balance and positioned across a church wall.

On one side of the scale, inside the church, sat the Apostle Paul; on the other side, outside the church, sat the devil. They each had a set of weights against which the good and bad deeds of newly-arrived souls could be measured. The apostle had weights which were 'shining like gold'; the devil had weights which were 'sooty and dark.' The souls approached the scale with great fear and trepidation, hoping they would be sent for purification in purgatory rather than damnation in hell.

'The weights estimated the deeds of each of the spirits according to the good or evil they had done,' Thurkill announced. 'When the balance inclined toward the apostle, he took that spirit and brought it through the eastern door, which was joined to the church, into the purifying fire to expiate its offences.

'When the balance inclined and shifted its weight toward the devil, he and his followers at once hurried the spirit away to eternal torment, wailing and cursing its father and mother for having begotten it. With huge grins they cast it into the deep and fiery furnace, which was at the feet of the devil who was weighing.'

Although there is no evidence of intercession or forgiveness in this exposition from Thurkill, both elements feature in the judgement scene over the entryway at Notre-Dame. They do so in the form of Mary and St. John, positioned on either side of Christ. Their purpose is to act as brokers of mercy, appealing for leniency on behalf of sinners, in the hope of counterbalancing any adverse outcome produced by the scales of justice.

Forgiveness, of course, is a prominent feature of Christianity. The act of forgiveness involving Jesus and the penitent thief, while on their respective crosses at Calvary, must be the most dramatic ever written down. All four gospels – Matthew, Mark, Luke and John – describe the general scene. With a backdrop of dark skies, Roman soldiers, disciples and family – and even, in the Gospel of Matthew, an earthquake – the slow, gruesome deaths of Jesus and the two malefactors, positioned to his left and right, are depicted.

Both thieves initially mocked Jesus, according to Matthew. Luke added to the story, describing how one of them repented and objected to the other's continued taunting: '"Don't you fear God," he said, "since you are under the same sentence? We are punished justly, for we are getting what our deeds deserve. But this man has done nothing wrong."' He then turned to Jesus and said: 'Jesus, remember me when you come into your kingdom.'

The repentant thief's statement was a clear declaration of his faith, accepting the claim of the man dying beside him to be the Son of God. It was also recognition of wrongdoings committed and a plea for forgiveness. According to Luke, forgiveness was immediately forthcoming. He remarked: 'Jesus answered him, "Truly I tell you, today you will be with me in paradise."'

This concept of heavenly mercy and compassion can be found in other religions, too, including Buddhism and Taoism. Perhaps the finest personification – or, more correctly, deification – of heavenly compassion in both these religions is the revered goddess Guanyin. Often referred to as the 'goddess of mercy', her role in the pantheon of deities is evident from the meaning of her name: 'observing the cries of the world'.

Various roles have been attributed to Guanyin, especially the relief of suffering. She promises to heed the cries and pleas of those who are troubled and to free them from their afflictions. Her ultimate goal also encompasses the liberating of souls from reincarnation or rebirth, thereby achieving salvation or nirvana.

Legend additionally has it that she once descended into the realms of hell and was so overcome by the pain and horrors she saw there that she released all the good karma she had built up in her lifetime, thus ensuring the freeing of many condemned souls.

Not surprisingly, given her penchant for empathy and great kindness, Guanyin has become a popular protector of women, children, the poor and the sick. In parts of Asia, she is believed to protect seamen and fishermen, and has been said to calm the sea when danger is imminent. She is also revered as a fertility goddess, helping those who wish to give birth to a child.

An interesting Ming statue of her, dated 1484, stands in the Lady Lever Art Gallery in Port Sunlight, Merseyside, which was established by the Lever family of soap fame. Her feet rest on lotus flowers set on the surface of a lake filled with the tears of the world. The inscription on the statue is to the point: 'She listens always.'

This feature of forgiveness is also evident in reports from those who undergo near-death experiences. It is worth our while examining two cases to establish the point. Both reveal similar patterns and share matching elements. Although they are separated by long periods of time – and are entirely unrelated to each other – the parallels between them are quite remarkable.

In 1986, a woman named Ann experienced an afterlife journey during a most difficult childbirth. She left her body and found herself travelling through a 'tunnel of bright lights.' Behind her was her physical body lying in the hospital; another part of her was moving away at great speed.

She was soon confronted by insights concerning her failings in life. 'I was shown that I wasn't great in life,' she remarked. 'To be more correct, I *knew* I wasn't great in life. I felt that I hadn't been perfectly God-fearing. The feeling was a general one. I hadn't done anything particularly dreadful. But I was human and I knew there were little things I had done that didn't merit whatever goodness was ahead. It was a terrorising feeling.'

Almost immediately she was overwhelmed by a profound sense of forgiveness. 'I was shown what I felt were words but I don't remember a voice,' she recalled. 'It was probably more like a feeling. It was a "knowing" that I was forgiven. It was like mercy being poured over me. All was forgiven and I knew it was. I felt, "After the life I have led, I'm forgiven and I'm going to heaven!" It was absolutely blissful. It was the most joyous thing that has ever happened to me. It was absolutely wonderful.'

She suddenly felt she was travelling backwards, away from what she perceived to be heaven. 'I would have stayed there if I could,' she remarked. 'I didn't think, "I have three children and a husband that I have to go back to." That didn't come into it. It was just that I was there and I was going to heaven.' The next thing, Ann was back in her body.

Let us immediately travel back some 1300 years to a different experience, this time described by St. Boniface, who was born in England but lived in Germany for many years. He recounted, in the early eighth century, the story of a man who departed from his body following an illness. 'He said that the extreme pain from a violent illness had suddenly freed his spirit from the burden of his body,' Boniface wrote. Just like Ann, the man found himself travelling away, 'high into the air.'

He, too, like Ann, found himself confronted by sins from his past life. 'He heard all his own sins, which he had committed from his youth on and had failed to confess or had forgotten or had not recognised as sins,' we are told. He had been vain, negligent and careless, stubborn and disobedient, a liar and sinner, and had boastfully put himself forward among men. The sins he heard were 'terrifying,' he recalled, using words almost identical to those used by Ann.

Immediately, just as in Ann's case, he was forgiven his sins. Angels were speaking out in his defence, pointing to his services to the weak, his kindness to the sick, his fasting, his praying, among many other virtues. 'The virtues,' he remarked, 'greatly magnified as they were, seemed to me far greater and more excellent than could ever have been practiced by my own strength.' He was then directed to 'return into his body at once,' which he did, completing a journey almost identical to Ann's 1300 years later.

In both stories we can identify the types of sins or life deeds that are assessed at the time of judgement. In Ann's case, she was confronted with the 'little things' she had done and the realisation that she hadn't been 'great in life,' certainly not virtuous enough to warrant any goodness that might lie ahead. In the St. Boniface story, the issues were more specific, although they still involved lower-level transgressions such as vanity, disobedience, stubbornness and negligence.

That minor matters such as these should have been singled out comes as no surprise. Contrary to what we might expect, the life review is not focused solely on the dark sins of our lives, such as murders or other grave deeds, although they are assessed, too. Our ordinary behaviours also matter. The way we have treated others, our self-obsession, our lack of compassion or concern – all the little things we have done – feature prominently.

One woman described how her selfishness was singled out. She was brought through specific happenings as if they were being highlighted for her to view. The events dated from the early years of her life right up to the present. It also seemed that how much she had learned in life – her quest for knowledge – was being stressed as important. All these flashbacks, she said, were coming at her at great speed, yet slow enough that she could take them all in.

Another woman spoke of reliving every event, emotion and thought from her life. In particular, she was shown how she related to others and how they related to her. There were feelings she was ashamed of; others that made her feel good. While witnessing all these images, she would comment to herself on how she might have done better. She felt unworthy, undeserving – not condemned, just not good enough to be in

137

God's presence. Her judgement ended well, however, with love, understanding and compassion being shown to her by God.

Yet another woman described how her life review included everything from the day she was born up to the time she died. All the events were in chronological order; everything she believed was important was there, including all her achievements. She was then shown her life once again, but this time from the viewpoint of God. The difference was stunning. Little things mattered – the kindness she showed to others; her charitable acts towards animals and those less well off than herself; in particular, anything she did that involved love. She, too, survived her ordeal.

Although these images pass by very quickly in terms of linear time – the time we measure things by on earth – they are relived during the experience exactly as they originally happened, with all the feelings and elements that pertained at the time. In the case of Monica, who we heard from earlier, she began her review while being wheeled at speed down a hospital corridor. Despite experiencing her events as if they were occurring again, when she returned to her physical body she was still being wheeled down the same corridor.

The pattern is similar in the case of Frank, who survived a near-drowning at the age of 14. In the time it took him to initially get into trouble to the time when he escaped from the water – probably a matter of a few minutes – he had witnessed many of the key events of his life.

'My life was being replayed before me,' Frank told me. 'It felt like everything was happening in sequence and I could recognise all the different events and seasons as they passed by. It was all in colour. The colour was fantastic. It was so vivid.

We still only had a black-and-white television in those days, so the colour amazed me.

'The images were from different times of the year. There was Christmas, summer holidays. My parents were there and my brothers and sisters were there. The scenes were mostly happening in the house where I was born and raised, but at 14 I had never really been anywhere else, so that's what you would expect. The last image was of me falling in the water.

'One of the images concerned summertime. We had a long back garden and I was sitting in it. It was really warm and sunny. I could see my mother coming out the back door. As she came out, everything was illuminated because of the colour. One or two of my brothers were in the yard.

'I have no idea why that image stands out, but for some reason it remains with me the most. It was probably insignificant to me when it happened originally, but seeing it again had a big impact and it sticks in my mind. I felt enthralled watching it, as I did with the other sequences.

'The whole thing went quick, but it also felt like it went on for hours. My brother, who was watching, said I was gone for five or six minutes. That was his concept of time, standing on the side, looking in. He said all the ripples were gone out of the water and he wasn't expecting me to come back.

'However, my two brothers and my friend, who were with me, were frozen with fear and had a longer view of time. They were younger than me and, when you are that young, time goes slower. Christmases never seem to come; they seem so far away. As you get older, they fly past. So it is possible that everything I saw only took place in milliseconds. The truth is the whole thing probably happened in the flick of a switch.'

All the stories recounted so far concern judgements described at the time of death. None of them relates to the Last Judgement, which some faiths – especially Christianity and Islam – profess will bring the final judgement of mankind. Many believe it will take place after the Second Coming of Christ, when 'the Son of Man comes in his glory, and all the angels with him, then he will sit on the throne of his glory.'

That excerpt comes from the Gospel of Matthew, which gives a vivid description of what is going to take place. In what will in effect be a final wrapping up of the fate of mankind, decisions will be made about the destination of the elect and sinners alike. 'All the nations will be gathered before him,' we are told, 'and he will separate people one from another as a shepherd separates the sheep from the goats.'

One of the most concise biblical passages ever written – Matthew 25:35-36 – then informs us of the qualities required to be saved: 'I was hungry and you gave me food, I was thirsty and you gave me something to drink, I was a stranger and you welcomed me, I was naked and you gave me clothing, I was sick and you took care of me, I was in prison and you visited me.' Those who meet these requirements will be told they will 'inherit the kingdom prepared for you from the foundation of the world.'

The precise opposite will apply to all those failing to meet those conditions. 'You that are accursed, depart from me into the eternal fire prepared for the devil and his angels,' they will be told. Although this notion of a last judgement – known as the Day of Resurrection or Day of Judgement in Islam – is an article of faith for Christians and Muslims, it is not the same as the immediate post-death judgement we have been talking about in this chapter.

The nature of these immediate post-death judgements, and why we need to prepare for them, will be referred to once again towards the end of this book. In the meantime, it is well worth returning to that famous book we encountered earlier – the Book of Life. This chronicle of life's deeds has worked its way into religious iconography and popular culture. It has appeared in art and poetry, as titles for books and movies, and as themes for psalms and hymns.

Among those hymns is the well-known *When the Roll is Called up Yonder*, which was composed by a Methodist from Pennsylvania named James Milton Black. Written in 1893, it was inspired by the non-attendance of a young girl at one of his Sunday school classes. He was surprised when she didn't respond to his roll call. Concerned for the child, he visited her home and discovered she had been ill with pneumonia.

Thinking it over, this Sunday school teacher was moved by a curious thought – wouldn't it be tragic if we weren't present, and didn't respond, when our names were called from the Book of Life after we die. On reaching home that day, he sat at his piano and instantly composed the hymn.

Not only did it end up becoming a huge international success, translated into numerous languages and used in an Academy Award-winning movie, but the hymn also encapsulates what we all hope will happen on the day we pass to the other side:

When the trumpet of the Lord shall sound, and time shall
* be no more,*
And the morning breaks, eternal, bright and fair;
When the saved of earth shall gather over on the other shore,
And the roll is called up yonder, I'll be there.

HELL

In the late nineteenth century, the American author Mark Twain scribbled the bare bones of a humorous anecdote about hell in his notebook. He would later use a fleshed-out version in a public speech. The anecdote went like this – a man is dying and given only two minutes to live. Worried about what he faces after death, he sends for a clergyman and asks: 'Where is the best place to go to?' The clergyman pauses, unsure of the most appropriate answer. 'Heaven for climate, hell for company,' he eventually says, pointing out that both places have their advantages!

That hell might contain a captivating – if grim – gallery of rogues, tyrants, vagabonds and raconteurs, with graphic stories and exotic tales to tell, is a reasonable presumption to make. Ivan the Terrible, Attila the Hun and Adolf Hitler rank among the many names you might expect to encounter, accompanied by any number of corrupt, evil, morally unsound, loathsome degenerates. You might also be surprised by those you recognise and know. Mark Twain explained the dilemma: 'I don't like to commit myself about heaven and hell, you see, I have friends in both places.'

You could be forgiven for thinking that Samuel Langhorne Clemens – better known as Mark Twain – might have been well-disposed to an afterlife in hell even when faced with the alternative of a sunny paradise. Should that be so, he would have been foolish. At least that is according to a vast array of first-hand accounts, literary depictions, vision insights and anecdotal evidence stretching back through the ages.

Just about every culture boasts a wide-ranging mythology, folklore or set of religious beliefs concerning hell. From the Hebrew bottomless pit named Abbadon, to the deep abyss of Greek mythology called Tartarus, through Tophet, Sheol, Hades, Naraka, the Islamic Jahannam and numerous other realms, it is clear that no other topic of human interest has been more extensively investigated and portrayed than the dark abode of evil that we may all end up in after we die.

Despite broad agreement that it is a place to avoid, the concept of hell familiar to most of the world today would be alien to our Old Testament ancestors. It wasn't that they had no image of punishment for sinners after death; they had. It was just that it differed from later imagery depicting scenes of blazing fire, unbearable heat and acrid smells, accompanied by physical torture, wailing, weeping and gnashing of teeth.

The Book of Daniel, which was written up to six centuries before Christ, gives us some idea of how our early forebears imagined hell. Unlike later images of a red-hot conflagration, the book described a place of 'shame and everlasting contempt.' Slightly later, Ecclesiastes – believed to date from the third century BC – implied that not only were there no fires but there was nothing at all, only extinction – 'neither working nor planning nor knowledge nor wisdom,' as the text put it.

It wasn't until Jesus made reference to a smouldering rubbish dump just below the old city walls of Jerusalem that the image of a fiery hell sprung to life. He never intended that the dump should be taken literally as the ultimate place of punishment or that its features were a replica of some blazing abode that existed elsewhere. Instead, he employed it as a useful metaphor indicating the sort of intensely undesirable prospects facing sinners after death.

The valley he referred to was known as Gehenna. It was here that the city's rubbish was discarded. The dump was a morass of filth and rotting waste, including the carcases of animals and corpses of criminals. It was infested with worms. Fires fanned by the addition of sulphur burned continuously in an effort to destroy the fermenting mass of detritus and decay.

Gehenna had an even darker history, being at one time a location where human sacrifices were made to the pagan god Moloch. Babies were burned alive, their loud screams stifled by drums, their parents forced to watch the barbarous scenes. By the time of Jesus, the dark and loathsome reputation of Gehenna was well-established. This together with its reputation as a fiery dump fostered Gehenna's image as the sort of place we would today call hell.

Jesus mentioned Gehenna many times, but he never referred to it as hell. Indeed, he would have been bemused to see Bible translators later transcribing Gehenna as 'hell', as the word itself is an eighth-century invention and didn't exist when he was alive. He would have been equally bemused at how widely – and literally – his allusions to a 'fiery hell', with its flames, smoke and stinking smells, would be copied and embellished over time.

Within two centuries of his death, the fiery imagery of hell alluded to by Jesus had blossomed into a blazing, raging maelstrom courtesy of the imaginations of early Church thinkers. Almost all of them, as we will shortly see, took huge liberties in what they wrote.

The images they created became so intense and terrifying that, even today, they colour the accounts of people who have hellish near-death experiences. Although their numbers are relatively small – with only around five per cent having negative encounters to report – right up to the present day some people describe blazing flames, a fiery hell, along with biblical-style depictions of the physical layout of the abode of the damned.

Eddie is one person who might know something about this place of eternal punishment, having travelled to its gates after temporarily dying a few years ago. Following an attempted suicide by drowning, he found himself outside of his body and witnessing what appeared to be heaven and hell. Although he brought back descriptions of both, his depiction of hell as a mountain-sized city of fire, enclosed by a wall, is compelling.

Eddie first described the wall. 'It was a very long, high wall, and it was light concrete in colour,' he informed me. 'My eyes followed the wall as it went up and up and up. I was in the sky, looking down at an angle of 45 degrees at this mountain-sized wall. It was really huge; mountain-sized, as I said.

'As my eyes reached the top of the wall, I saw the fire. There were no flames, just the darkest-looking fire several feet above the top of the wall. On top of the fire there were large circles of thick, black, oily smoke. Afterwards I would think of this as a huge walled city of fire.

'I wasn't frightened at the time; I was just there, looking at it. What I thought about most of all was the size of it. It's not possible for me to describe how big it was. I was sky-high, really high; and this wall, when it started to take shape, I couldn't see the end of it. It was so long and mountain-sized.

'I now ask: "Why was the city there?" For accountability, I suppose, for people who committed horrendous things in this life. There has to be accountability for certain things. I think there will have to be answers. Maybe the walled city has something to do with that.'

Eddie's hellish experience is both menacing and intense – the bubbling cauldron of fire, the oily black smoke, the interminable and impenetrable wall, the threat of damnation for those condemned to inhabit this terrifying place as punishment for their transgressions and sins.

The imagery is gloomy and threatening, redolent of extreme suffering, agony and pain. Not only does the scene promise anguish and distress, but it also lets us know that there will be no escape. Enter this walled citadel of fire-filled doom and you are there for eternity, condemned to the flames of hell.

What Eddie describes replicates the picture of hell developed by thinkers dating back to the years shortly after the death of Christ. Among religious scholars and philosophers of the time was the controversial Cyprian of Carthage, who insisted that 'the damned will burn forever in hell. Devouring flames will be their eternal portion.' There was also the Christian author Tertullian who within 170 years of the crucifixion wrote a book *De Spectaculis*, which contained extraordinary hellish embellishment and overstatement.

Commenting on how he would feel at the final judgement, Tertullian remarked: 'How shall I admire, how laugh, how rejoice, how exult, when I behold so many proud monarchs groaning in the lowest abyss of darkness; so many magistrates liquefying in fiercer flames than they ever kindled against the Christians; so many sage philosophers blushing in red-hot fires with their deluded pupils; so many tragedians more tuneful in the expression of their own sufferings; so many dancers tripping more nimbly from anguish than ever before from applause.'

By the late sixth century, exaggerated fiery depictions of hell were being endorsed and articulated by a more substantial, authoritative religious figurehead – Pope Gregory I, who was one of the esteemed fathers of Christianity. When writing his *Dialogues* in 593 and 594, he certainly didn't hold back on the graphic prose, describing sinners being thrown into hellfire, once mighty men of this world hanging in flames, wrongdoers being sentenced to everlasting torments, and sulphuric rivers sweeping away the damned.

Warming to his theme, he outlined how just as the good in heaven have no end to their joys so also the wicked have no release from their torments. How was he so certain of this? Because, he said, the Bible showed that God rained fire and brimstone on the men of Sodom and Gomorrah as retribution for their deviant sexual practices, ensuring that 'fire might burn them and the stench of brimstone smother and kill them.' He deduced that God uses similar sanctions to punish other sinners.

Pope Gregory I, although a great organiser and pragmatist, required a philosopher of substance to endorse his reflections and validate his thoughts. He found just the man in the form of St. Augustine of Hippo. Not only did he live in a similar era to Gregory, in the broadest sense – dying about 100 years before Gregory was born – but he produced a vast library of theological works defending Christianity. One of the most important of these books was *The City of God*, which not only examined the case for hell but provided elaborate support for its worst excesses.

St. Augustine possessed a powerful intelligence and was an ardent believer in the primacy of punishment. Those condemned to hell, he wrote in *The City of God*, 'shall certainly be pained by the fire.' Drawing from scripture – including a remark by Jesus concerning the damned to the effect that 'their worm shall not die, neither shall their fire be quenched' – he concluded that 'it is absurd to suppose that either body or soul will escape pain in the future punishment.'

St. Augustine's theological conclusions co-joined with Pope Gregory I's more flowery prose copper-fastened the case for the fiery hell which dominated not only Church thinking, but virtually *all* thinking, for the next 1,600 years. This sort of fiery, colourful imagery peaked during the medieval period, stretching from the fifth to the fifteenth centuries. Those were dark and difficult times, full of death, disease, famine and war. Religion was about the only thing that kept people going, exercising their imaginations and controlling their bleak lives.

Sermons were the popular – and often the only – entertainment available. Uneducated peasants flocked to churches to hear them. Preachers, with their arms aloft and cassocks flowing, sermonised about scorching, oven-like infernos, full of burnings, floggings and grotesque devilish creatures. Their flocks cowered before them, horrified by the sizzling, blistering punishment they faced. It was perfect material for evangelists to deal with – easy to articulate yet terrifying for those on the receiving end.

We can imagine the faithful dropping to their knees, weeping and begging forgiveness when confronted with the sort of red-hot conflagration described by the following medieval Italian preacher: 'Fire, fire! That is the recompense for your perversity, you hardened sinners. Fire, fire, the fires of hell! Fire in your eyes, fire in your mouth, fire in your guts, fire in your throat, fire in your nostrils, fire inside and fire outside, fire beneath and fire above, fire in every part. Ah, miserable folk! You will be like rags burning in the middle of this fire.'

Accounts of hellish visions, based on allegedly true-life visits to heaven and hell, were also popular during medieval times. One of the best known concerns an Irish monk and has been dated to the seventh century. The monk in question, Furseus or 'Fursey', was 'led forth from the body' having been attacked by a 'bodily infirmity,' according to the Anglo-Saxon monk and scholar Bede in his *Ecclesiastical History of the English People*.

On his travels Furseus witnessed what Bede described as 'the very great struggle and toil of the accursed spirits.' He saw these condemned souls flying through the flames of hell. They shouted accusations and falsehoods against him. At one stage, the unclean spirits caught a condemned man who was burning in the fire and threw him at Furseus, resulting in his shoulder and cheek being burned. Legend has it that he retained the burn marks on his shoulder and cheek for the rest of his life.

Another colourful vision story, which appeared towards the close of the twelfth century, concerned 'the monk of Evesham Abbey' who became ill and died only to return to life with an extraordinary story to tell. We are informed how, on the monk's re-entry to his body – just as his fellow friars were about to assemble for their midnight mass – 'his eyelids began to quiver slightly. After a short while a moisture, like tears, began to flow gently over his cheeks, and, as anyone might cry in one's sleep, he seemed to utter frequent sighs.' He then began to tell his tale.

The monk's vivid description of hell was of a stinking lake surrounded by two promontories – one boiling hot, the other intensely cold. As for the souls crowded there, 'their punishment was first to be dipped in the fetid lake; then, breaking away from there, they were devoured by volumes of flame that met them; and finally, in swinging balls of fire, like sparks from a furnace, they were tossed on high and then fell to the bottom of the other bank.'

Oscillating back and forth, they moved from hot to cold, savouring 'the stench of the lake and the burnings of the raging fire.' We can only conjecture how humble, poorly-educated medieval farm labourers, out for their regular Sunday service, would sit in open-mouthed horror at this appalling tale!

Apart from preachers' overblown orations, the only other medieval entertainments were annual pageants or plays where huge torture-friendly cauldrons, firecrackers, smoke bombs, flaming sulphur and the sounds of pots and pans were used to replicate the horrors of hell. People loved them; the Church, with an eye on control through fear, loved them, too. Church leaders also savoured the paintings, wall reliefs and frescoes portraying brutal hell-like tortures that adorned the walls of churches, reminding the faithful of the consequences of even the mildest slip.

These images were dramatic, to say the least. Their grisly, spine-chilling illustrations depicted cauldrons of fire, horrifying creatures, hideous devils and souls being tortured, which left little to the imagination of illiterate churchgoers. Sometimes this artwork was positioned on the wall close to the exit door to ensure that those departing would carry dark images of the afterlife with them on their way home.

It was also customary for so-called 'doom' paintings – representing Christ surrounded by hell on one side, heaven on the other – to be exhibited in churches to hammer home to the faithful the stark options facing them at the time of their deaths. Perhaps the best-known example is *The Last Judgement*, by Michelangelo, which can be seen in the Sistine Chapel. Similar dark images of hell appeared in the literature of the time, most notably in Dante's *Inferno*, which I will more comprehensively refer to in the chapter on The Prince of Darkness.

It was inevitable that the primacy of a fiery hell, with its exaggerated tortures and fierce punishments, would eventually be questioned and undermined, and it was. The first sea change in attitudes towards a grim hellish afterlife can be traced to the post-medieval Renaissance and its focus on humanism. This new philosophy – and mode of living – emphasised the primary importance of the individual over the collective; the role of the secular over religion; the importance of reason, education and scientific inquiry over blind belief in God.

During the Renaissance, which came to life in the fourteenth century and lasted until the seventeenth century, people took a greater interest in money and in the enjoyable things in life. Human fulfilment in this world, and not in the next, suddenly mattered. Belief in the potential of the individual replaced the belief that we only survive in this world as preparation for our true destiny after death.

While early believers may have embraced the concept of extreme afterlife punishment and agonising damnation, their Renaissance and post-Renaissance counterparts took a more tolerant view. To them, it seemed downright wrong that a just and loving God would stand idly by and observe the sort of dire punishments described in earlier times. It was equally difficult to credit that angels and saints might take pleasure in the sight of sinners being tortured in the fires of hell.

This bizarre idea of observing the sufferings of others being a heavenly reward was at one time widely promoted. The hugely influential churchman St. Augustine had expressed the view that the saints in heaven would continually acquaint themselves with 'the eternal sufferings of the lost.' St. Thomas Aquinas developed the point, arguing that 'the happiness of the saints may be more delightful to them' because they were 'allowed to see perfectly the sufferings of the damned.'

The twelfth-century theologian Peter Lombard was notably more extreme, saying that the elect, on seeing the torments of the impious, would be 'satiated with joy.' These harsh viewpoints raised some genuinely disturbing questions. Would a mother elevated to heaven rejoice in the torments and tortures of her child in the fires of hell? Would a husband or wife relish seeing his or her spouse enduring the traumas and distress of everlasting damnation? How could a fair and kind God allow such horrific scenarios to arise? He couldn't, many argued.

The issue of who was responsible for sinful behaviour was reviewed, too. While early societies pointed the finger directly at the offender, their later counterparts wondered if the offender might have been influenced by factors such as family upbringing or inherited traits. Punishing people for things they did without being directly responsible for them seemed unfair.

A further issue also came into play – the notion that people can be redeemed and reformed. Instead of just being punished, people should be rehabilitated, this view held. Retribution was replaced by reformation. These new perspectives began to appear not only in various societies but in their many religions, too. As a result, the commonly-held belief in a harrowing hell full of suffering and pain was soon on the way out.

Another nail in its coffin was the belief that a sinner's death might be followed not by punishment but by extinction and nothingness. This notion wasn't necessarily connected to any growing disbelief in God or an afterlife. Instead, it was linked to a controversial interpretation of the Bible to the effect that the souls of the damned, following death, are annihilated and disintegrate into nothing at all.

There was ample evidence supporting this view in the Bible. Jesus clearly refers to the possible destruction of both body and soul in hell when he says: 'Do not fear those who kill the body but cannot kill the soul. Rather fear him who can destroy both soul and body in hell.' This allusion to destruction – implying obliteration or wiping out – was far removed from the established concept of 'everlasting fire' and 'eternal punishment'.

Yet another passage – this time from the Book of Malachi, which is the final book of the Old Testament – provides further support for extinction when it says, regarding the wicked, how the day is coming which will 'set them on fire' and 'not a root or a branch will be left to them.' In addition, the substantial number of occasions where God uses the words 'perish', 'destroy' or 'destruction' when referring to punishment of the unjust implies a hell involving something entirely different from an eternity of everlasting anguish.

References such as these prompted questioning of the understanding of hell among Christians, leading some to believe that, whatever about eternal life in heaven, punishment – if it exists at all – will not be everlasting in hell. Although a major, controversial issue, it too has helped undermine the long-established view of a never-ending, blazing, burning punishment for sinners.

The concept of a fiery hell never disappeared, however, and the conventions of blazing fires and horrific creatures continued to feature in world religions, including Christianity. Islam's hell

– known as Jahannam, the Arabic derivative of Gehenna – has its fire, blazing flames, pitch-black smoke, scalding water and desperate agonies for those condemned to eternal damnation. Should wrongdoers ask for respite, they are showered with molten copper and lashed with iron rods, the Koran tells us.

Hinduism and Buddhism also have their hells. The Hindu equivalent contains many severe punishments including being cooked alive in boiling oil, forced to drink molten iron, beaten with whips and obliged to eat disgusting things such as pus, urine and excreta. Torments of the various hells of Buddhism include being roasted in blazing ovens, having flesh ravaged by animals, or being sliced into pieces.

Perhaps because these dramatic images have been set in stone for so long a time – in Christianity, Islam, Hinduism and Buddhism – similar apocalyptic images continue to form the backdrop of at least some reports brought back by those who have undergone near-death experiences. They are occasionally mentioned even in modern times.

Bill Wiese recounts a remarkable modern-day, yet very old-fashioned, experience in his book *23 Minutes in Hell*. His story dates to 23 November 1998, when he embarked on a terrifying journey. At the centre of the hell he entered there was an enormous pit filled with raging flames, within which condemned souls lived a life of torment. Their screams filled the air. Without rest or sleep, consumed by thirst and hopelessness, they were in despair and on the edge of insanity.

This appalling world was also full of grotesque creatures, variously described as having deformed bodies, gigantic teeth, sunken eyes, razor-like claws and sharp protruding fins. Some of these horrible creatures patrolled the perimeter of the pit, preventing escape. Everywhere there was fire, smoke and foul smells. Having eventually broken free from this scene of damnation, Wiese arrived in God's presence and devoted himself, on his return to life, to relating what he saw to others.

A no less disturbing hell was experienced by the 28-year-old businessman Matthew Botsford after his heart stopped three times following a random shooting incident in 1992. He quickly found himself in the realm of hell. While there, he was suspended in midair, his arms outstretched, his wrists and ankles manacled by chains, his body hanging over a glowing red abyss. Smoke rose from smouldering lava, which seemed to Matthew to contain lost souls. He heard their loud screams of anguish and despair.

Time and again he felt his skin being burnt to the bone, only for it to re-form and be burnt again. He was also attacked by demons, who ripped off his skin with their sharp teeth, causing intense pain. Although he felt that the torment would last forever, he was eventually rescued by what he described as the 'hand of God.' His story was recounted by his wife, Nancy, in her book *A Day in Hell: Death to Life to Hope*, which not only described Matthew's experience but their newly-found faith.

Despite reports such as these, the notion of a hell based on material fire and eternal burning had lost its vital force by the end of the twentieth century and no longer controlled the imagination of the faithful as it once did. The concept was replaced by an understanding of hell involving separation from God. Rather than a place, it was understood to be more a disturbing state of existence without God and, to this end, reflected one aspect of the reports brought back by those who had near-death experiences.

This feature of being excluded from the presence of God was articulated by many temporary-death survivors I spoke to. One man I interviewed, named Edward, who had briefly died during a life-threatening operation, expressed the point well. 'I think hell is being in a position where there is something preventing you from seeing God's face,' he explained. A woman described afterlife punishment as being 'an absence from God.' Many others who had travelled to the borders of death, yet later returned to life, expressed this view, too.

Underpinning what they said was the intense desire to be in the company of the all-loving God, or 'superior being', they encountered on their journeys to the other side. Denied this closeness, they felt ostracised, unwanted, rejected or ignored, with all the attendant feelings of horror and fear that this sense of being shut out produced. The psychological damage felt by those who had died was immense. That the exclusion might stretch to eternity was more distressing still.

A close study of ancient texts reveals that Jesus and those compiling the Old and New Testaments were fully aware of the fearful power of exclusion. In the Old Testament we can see many examples where God is described as deliberately rejecting, or 'excluding', those who have acted against him. In the Book of Deuteronomy – written some six or seven centuries before Christ – we read how if anyone turns away from the Lord, 'the Lord shall blot out his name.'

In the Book of Jeremiah – written around the same time – God tells those who have sinned against him: 'I will cast you, and the city which I gave you and your fathers, out of my presence.' In the Book of Exodus – written a little later – he is seen to repeat this threat, saying: 'Whoever has sinned against me, I will blot him out of my book.' The idea of transgressors being 'cut off' featured strongly in these pre-Christian writings.

This form of mental punishment, consisting of what might be called 'the horror of being excluded from God', is also seen in the words of Christ in the Gospels. It is referred to in many places, most notably towards the end of the Sermon on the Mount. While contrasting true faith with spurious faith, Jesus pointed out that many who thought they were doing good deeds may have been acting only for their own advantage. To those, he warned that on judgement day the Lord would say: 'I never knew you, away from me, you evildoers.' This threat he repeated on other occasions.

A second psychological factor which has often been ignored or neglected due to the emphasis on a fiery hell is the concept of 'torment'. For people who undergo temporary death, torment consists mainly of mental suffering, agony or pain. Just as in the case of exclusion, it is of psychological and not physical significance. In that sense, it has great relevance to what might happen at, or after, the point of death.

Torment is widely reported among those who have negative near-death experiences. The sensation sometimes results from mind-numbingly repetitive actions which transgressors are often forced to undertake. This feature is evident in the following story of a man, David, who left his body during major heart surgery and travelled to the other side. His story, which I have referred to in other books, is one of the most disturbing I have ever encountered.

'All of a sudden I was standing in a field and I could see over the hills and mountains,' David told me. 'I could see for miles and miles in all directions, right over the horizon. There was no colour, everything was black and white. There was no green or anything like that.

'Everything was really gloomy. On the ground there was nothing but muck and millions and millions of bodies climbing under and over each other. It was like in formation – first under a body and then over a body, climbing through muck. It was like a grey mess, everything was covered in mud.

'It was being communicated to me that that was what I was going to have to do – climb under a body and over a body. I was very distraught. I thought I was in hell or someplace, although we are led to believe that hell is all fire. I felt traumatised about what was happening to me.

'I honestly felt it was happening. I was getting ready to do it. I saw a woman stand up, as if she was a supervisor in charge of these bodies. I only saw her from the back. The mud was dripping off her when she stood up. The woman was dressed but covered in mud. It was very vivid.

'I thought to myself, "Have I to do this forever? Am I someplace where this is me for the rest of eternity?" Just at that, a big, coarse voice roared at me from the heavens. It said, "Get out! Get out and save some souls!" I eventually came out of the coma.'

The torment of eternal repetition, just outlined – invariably occurring with grim, hideous landscapes as a backdrop – is not uncommonly reported by the small number of people who have hellish experiences. We can see in their stories the tiresome, unvarying, literally soul-destroying activities that the condemned are obliged to perform. What is worse is the understanding that these mind-numbing rituals will last forever.

Features similar to these are evident in the story of George Ritchie, the American who died temporarily in December 1943 from an extreme bout of pneumonia and who we encountered earlier in this book. Ritchie, too, witnessed a vast, crowded plain filled with enormous numbers of beings. Thousands were present, all of them frustrated, angry and miserable.

Instead of climbing under and over other bodies – as seen in the previous example – these unfortunate souls appeared to be repetitively gouging, punching and kicking one another in a frenzy of impotent rage. Although it seemed they were involved in fights to the death, no one died. Blows were never landed, intended targets never touched, and the resulting anger felt by each soul was intense.

The similarities between the two narratives – George Ritchie's and David's – are readily apparent: the tedious process of doing the same things over and over again, the endless frustration, the torment, and the notion of a hell involving the wrecking of the mind and the emotions. It is this poisonous, insidious nature of eternal condemnation that stands out, and it is no surprise to discover that similar descriptions stretch back into the dark recesses of time.

Back in the eighth century – approximately 1,200 years before David or George Ritchie had their bleak experiences – we find remarkably similar hellish features recounted by the Anglo-Saxon monk and scholar Bede in his *Ecclesiastical History of the English People*. These descriptions concern a Northumbrian man, Drythelm, who died early one night from a serious illness but who revived at dawn.

Drythelm, who was accompanied on his journey by a guide, witnessed a place featuring tedious, painful, repetitive patterns. Balls of fire rose out of a great pit, each one full of men's spirits. These 'masses of black flames' would rise up only to fall back down again, over and over, in repetitive motion. They were 'cast up on high' like 'ashes ascending with smoke', after which, as the fiery vapour contracted, they 'slipped back once more to the abyss at the bottom.' This pattern was repeated indefinitely.

With the backdrop of a foul smell, sounds of lamentation and mourning, allied to the 'cackling laughter' of the souls' captors, it was apparent to Drythelm that he had witnessed hell. It was later confirmed by his guide that what he had seen was 'the mouth of hell's torment, and whatever man at any time falls into it is never rescued from it throughout eternity.'

So far, I have identified three negative states associated with the death process – a feeling of exclusion or being rejected, a feeling of intense torment, and a feeling of restless agitation. These states involve emotions including anguish, unhappiness, suffering, hopelessness and despair. All these feelings generate significant distress and are commonly shared by people who go through 'hellish' temporary deaths. Many describe them as representing the essence of hell.

These punishments are highly disturbing in their own right, even if they are light years removed from the concept of a fiery hell propagated down through the ages. The impact on the person who is dying can be equally traumatic. The sense of horror and terror can be just as profound. What this implies – why it happens and what the implications are for life after death – I will examine at the end of this book.

In the meantime, before concluding this chapter, it is worth returning to Mark Twain to hear more of his views concerning hell, a few of which were alluded to earlier. Despite the bleak and cheerless descriptions of hell we have seen so far – many of which must have been known to this well-informed author

– we might ask whether he feared being condemned to eternal damnation. The truth is, we really don't know.

What we do know, however, is the view of hell he chose for his famous fictional character Huckleberry Finn. Faced with helping the runaway slave Jim, or handing him in to his owner, the young Huckleberry was confronted with a big dilemma. To avoid 'being lost and going to hell,' he wrote a letter identifying where the slave was hiding and how he could be recaptured for a reward. He put the letter to one side.

Then he started to ponder: 'Thinking over our trip down the river; and I see Jim before me, all the time; in the day, and in the night-time, sometimes moonlight, sometimes storms, and we a floating along, talking and singing, and laughing.' He thought how good Jim was, how he was so grateful for being helped to escape, how he said, 'I was the best friend old Jim ever had in the world, and the only one he's got now; and then I happened to look around, and see that paper.'

Huckleberry lifted up the letter, knowing he had a choice to make. 'I was trembling,' he recalled, 'because I'd got to decide, forever, betwixt two things, and I knowed it. I studied a minute, sort of holding my breath, and then says to myself: "All right, then, I'll go to hell" – and tore it up.....as long as I was in, and in for good, I might as well go the whole hog.' All things considered, Huckleberry Finn might have made a wise decision!

THE PRINCE OF
DARKNESS

S et in the dark recesses of hell sits a beast, black like a
raven, with clawed feet, a great beak, resting on an iron
chair positioned over a blazing fire. His tail is long and
sharp. A multitude of demons surrounds him. The stench of
smoke and sulphur fills the air. 'What is this monster's name?'
the anxious visitor asks his guide. 'This beast whom you see is
called Lucifer,' comes the sombre reply.

It could be the opening scene of a horror movie, designed to
strike terror and fear into audiences cowering in their seats. It
might, alternatively, be part of a nightmare. Instead, it was one
of the many horrifying images of hell contained in the over-
stated and exaggerated twelfth-century manuscript *The Vision
of Tundale*.

'Come therefore and I will show you the greatest adversary
of the human race,' Tundale, a valiant Irish knight who had
temporarily died, was told by his angel guide. What he eventually
saw struck fear into readers far and wide. Had there been a
twelfth-century bestseller list, the book – which was soon
translated into 15 languages – would have topped it by a mile.
Even by modern standards, this was a potboiler of note.

'This horrible monster had no less than a thousand hands,'
Tundale reported, 'and each hand was a thousand cubits long
and ten cubits wide.' There were 20 fingers to each hand, and
each had long claws containing 1,000 points. The claws were

made of iron. Circling above him were innumerable souls of the dead.

Beneath Lucifer's iron seat was a blazing fire fanned by bellows. As it burned, he 'turned himself from one side to the other side in very great wrath, and he stretched out all his hands into the multitude of souls and then compressed them.' All the souls were either dismembered or deprived of head, feet or hands. Then, by just breathing, he inhaled and exhaled the souls into different parts of hell.

There was a time when life was a lot more uplifting for this colourful character named Lucifer. He was once the finest of angels, beautiful, wise and perfect in every way. He had 'the seal of perfection,' the Book of Ezekiel tells us in what scholars believe was a passage referring to him. 'You were in Eden, the garden of God; every precious stone was your covering: the ruby, the topaz and the diamond; the beryl, the onyx and the jasper; the lapis lazuli, the turquoise and the emerald; and the gold,' Ezekiel informs us.

Unfortunately, we are informed, pride brought the downfall of Lucifer. Although occupying a position of privilege and power, his vanity and ambition overcame him. He wanted to be God. The Book of Isaiah outlines his ambitions: 'Thou hast said in thine heart, I will ascend into heaven, I will exalt my throne above the stars of God: I will sit also upon the mount of the congregation, in the sides of the north: I will ascend above the heights of the clouds; I will be like the most high.'

Instead, Lucifer was cast out of heaven, 'cut down to the ground'. From then on, this 'son of the morning' became the 'prince of darkness', 'the evil one', 'the prince of demons', and the facilitator of all that would bring sin into our lives. He is variously referred to as Satan, Beelzebub, Leviathan, Antichrist, Belial or, quite simply, 'the Devil,' although, as is always the case in these matters, there are disputes over who these many entities might be. We can safely say, however, that Lucifer was the ultimate shining star who fell from the sky only to land alongside us here on earth.

By the time Tundale was said to have witnessed him in the twelfth century, this 'prince of darkness' had evolved into a beast of horrific and grotesque proportions. Although the Bible says nothing about his looks – apart from telling us that he disguises himself as an 'angel of light' – it didn't stop the febrile imaginations of successive generations from conjuring up a composite picture that was truly unsightly.

The horns were borrowed from Scandinavian gods; the hoofs and goat hair were appropriated from Pan, the Greek god of shepherds and flocks. The pitchfork was stolen from the Greek deity Pluto, ruler of the underworld. Bats provided the wings. Even the fiery hell he inhabited was acquired from a reference Jesus made to the smouldering rubbish dump called Gehenna, as we saw in the chapter on hell.

By the fifth century, many of the devil's dark attributes were already in place. In 447, the Council of Toledo was in a position to provide the Church's official account of his features. They didn't hold back, describing him as 'a large, black, monstrous apparition with horns on his head, cloven hoofs – or one cloven hoof – ass's ears, hair, claws, fiery eyes, terrible teeth, an immense phallus, and a sulphurous smell.' He was clearly not a pretty sight!

Eerie traditions spread far and wide. It was believed that either the devil or his fellow demons might pop in through your mouth when you sneezed; hence the tradition of saying 'God bless you.' Because he was frequently depicted in red, people with red hair were considered to be touched by the devil. Again, because he was often shown to be left-handed – *sinister* being the Latin for 'left' – left-handed people, at one time, were considered to be evil.

His psychological profile was equally unappealing. The Bible told us that he was 'the father of lies', a schemer, deceiver, tempter and a hoodwinker who distorts the truth and leads us astray. The ultimate Antichrist, he sows evil and blinds our minds so that we cannot see the light. As the antithesis of God, he personifies all that is dark and venomous, dishonourable and corrupt.

The Bible also told us that he has been hanging around as long as mankind, if not longer. He was said to have been in the Garden of Eden, where he masqueraded as the serpent who whispered in Eve's ear that she should eat from the tree of knowledge. He was also mentioned in the Book of Job – probably the most ancient text of the Old Testament and certainly the most beautifully written – where he was responsible for Job being afflicted with 'painful sores from the soles of his feet to the crown of his head.'

Although many of these grim features of Lucifer were already securely in place by the fifth century, it wasn't until medieval times that the truly shocking, hideous, nightmarish depictions of this beast of hell were refined and established. Much of the credit for this was due to the German mystic Mechthild of Magdeburg, who was a nun of noble lineage and whose visions were chronicled in her little-known work *The Flowing Light of the Godhead*, written between 1250 and 1280.

Mechthild spared little in her descriptions. Lucifer, she said, 'sits bound by his guilt in the deepest abyss.' All the sins, torments, sickness and shame in which hell, purgatory and the earth are so wretchedly entangled flow from his fiery heart and mouth. His hell 'roars and rages,' while the souls there stew and roast, swimming and wading in the stench and morass among the serpents and in the mire.

Christians parade before him, naked and terrified as they await punishment. He grabs the proud ones and thrusts them under his tail, saying, 'I have not sunk so deep that I shall not lord it over you.' Sodomites pass down his throat and live in his belly; when he draws breath they are pulled into his belly, but when he coughs they are pushed out again.

He places hypocrites on his lap and kisses them grotesquely, saying: 'You are my equals.' Those who have been unchaste lie bound together before Lucifer; but if one of them arrives alone then the devil becomes his mate.

On and on Mechthild went. Murderers stand before Lucifer, covered in blood, and receive blows from a sword. Misers are devoured by Lucifer, who then excretes them from under his tail. The gluttonous are forced to stand hungry before him and eat burning stones and drink sulphur and pitch.

Not surprisingly, Mechthild told us that she was so overcome by the experience – primarily the stench and the heat – that she 'could neither sit up nor walk' and was deprived of her five senses for three days. Hers was a torrid vision of Hell!

It would be hard not to notice the similarity between the Mechthild depiction of Lucifer's hell and the depiction featured in Dante's *Inferno*, which was set in the year 1300 but written a little later. No more than half a century, or so, separated the two texts. It has been suggested – correctly, it seems, from an analysis of the two manuscripts – that Dante in his *The Divine Comedy*, which *Inferno* was part of, took many of his cues from his predecessor.

Dante's no-holds-barred description of the horrors of hell was full of images that can only be regarded as gruesome. Fortune tellers and false prophets have their heads put on backwards. 'Backward it behoved them to advance, as to look forward had been taken from them,' he noted, this punishment being inflicted because they wished to see too far ahead. A further huge collection of sinners, including flatterers who are steeped in excrement, receive some of the most horrendous punishments imaginable.

At the heart of Dante's hell we meet Lucifer with his three faces, six eyes and mighty bat-like wings. Encased in ice, but visible from the mid-breast upwards, he chews on three sinners with his different mouths. Two of the sinners are Brutus and Cassius, who were involved in the assassination of Caesar; they are stuffed feet-first in Lucifer's jaws.

The third sinner is Judas Iscariot, who betrayed Jesus; he is stuffed head-first inside Lucifer's middle mouth. For his sins, Judas has his back stripped of all skin by Lucifer's claws. Between them, these images justified the infamous inscription Dante saw on the gates of hell: 'Abandon all hope, you who enter here.'

John Bunyan, the seventeenth-century English author and preacher, provided equally gruesome images following his journey to hell. He described an odious landscape, full of horrific smells, echoing with sounds of torment and suffering. One woman he saw was being force-fed flaming sulphur. Two other souls were being plunged in liquid fire and burning brimstone.

His ears, he remarked, were 'filled with the horrid yellings of the damned spirits.'

Bunyan topped off his description of hell with a chilling depiction of Lucifer sitting on a burning throne in a sulphurous lake of liquid fire, 'his horrid eyes sparkling with hellish fury.' There he sat, spewing 'horrid blasphemies' against God, with every poisonous utterance intensifying the heat of hell. This image alone was worthy of the writing skills of Dante!

The fiery language and gruesome descriptions provided by Bunyan in the seventeenth century in many ways marked the end of an era. Although Bible-thumpers and inflamed sermonisers never let go of the devil's dark image, general public perceptions were about to change abruptly. The catalyst for change was no less than the English poet John Milton, whose epic creation *Paradise Lost* was published in 1667.

'Better to reign in Hell than serve in Heaven,' Satan declares in what was a surprisingly sympathetic literary treatment of this fallen angel. Not only did the poem portray him as tragic and proud, but he was also revealed to be majestic and heroic, defiantly opposed to a tyrannical God. Although still thoroughly evil, the new Lucifer was many steps removed from the hideous, nightmarish figure of old.

The cloven hoofs, however, never entirely went away. Fast-forward to 1958, when it was reported that Lucifer put in an appearance at Tooreen dancehall in County Mayo, Ireland. Run by Fr. James Horan, who set up Knock Airport, the rules in the venue were simple and clear – no cheek-to-cheek dancing. It wasn't always a popular or well-respected rule.

One evening, a stranger arrived, smooth and handsome, who caught all the girls' eyes. He was an intimate and suggestive dancer. There was a whiff of danger about him. He left with a local girl in hand, his chauffeur-driven car pulling up to collect them outside. On entering the car, she noticed he had a cloven hoof and fled for her life.

The event sparked a run of similar appearances in other Irish dancehalls. Among them was an appearance in Mallow, where a girl said she witnessed cloven hoofs on a man who had asked her to step outside. The well-known showband Joe Dolan and the Drifters decided to capitalise on the event by announcing themselves as 'the red devils of entertainment' for their Mallow visit a few days later. The stunt backfired; instead of the expected crowd of 2000, less than 500 turned up.

In 1990 a new variation of the story surfaced in Porto Velho, Brazil. This time the venue was a bar where a competition was being held to establish the best performer of the lambada, a frowned-upon and sexually-suggestive dance. A slender male, suitably resplendent in black attire, caught every female's eyes. All the women wanted to dance with him. Suddenly, a loud scream was heard and a girl fainted.

Later, the girl described how, when dancing with the man, she looked and saw he had a demon's features and flaming eyes. Not only had he disappeared after she screamed, but he had left in his wake the scent of sulphur. Soon, it would seem, this individual appeared at other Brazilian dance venues where he displayed similar silken skills.

Other manifestations of this same demon turned up in the USA, Mexico and Saudi Arabia – the latter providing a most unusual variation of the tale. Here, two young ladies peeped into a venue where stylish, beautiful – and, most significantly, unveiled – women were dancing. The young ladies were enticed inside. To their horror, one of them spotted that the unveiled dancers had the legs and hoofs of a donkey. Thankfully, no such legs had been spotted on the females of County Mayo!

Bible readers would hardly be surprised by these stories, especially considering the devil's capacity for disguise. For someone who we are told can impersonate 'an angel of light', it would be no great hardship to turn up as a seductive lady-killer in the ballrooms of romance. Filled with lustful young hopefuls, there could be no better hunting ground for this evil being who, it is said, 'prowls around like a roaring lion, seeking someone to devour.'

Apart from occasional sightings such as those enumerated above, the idea of a hideous, gruesome, terrifying devil, acting as the personification of evil has faded even more in modern times. As a consequence, Lucifer, with his cloven hoofs and horns, has largely had his day. His physical persona no longer walks among us, trampling all over us, prompting us and leading us to perform nasty deeds. As the eminent Harvard psychologist Henry Murray put it, he has become 'a ludicrous ham actor' with no greater part to play in man's imagination than his appendix.

Not that the power of evil has disappeared; to the contrary, man's seemingly unlimited capacity to perform acts of evil is still very much there. It is just that it is perceived differently, mainly as coming from within us and not from a man with cloven hoofs. Perhaps this view was best put by Oscar Wilde when he said: 'We are each our own devil, and we make this world our hell.' His observation will resonate more with us when we come to the final chapter.

What we will discover there is that, in truth, the devil is an imaginary creature who sits on our shoulder while prompting us to commit dark deeds, the consequences of which we carry with us beyond death. He represents the black side to all of us, provoking us and inciting us to act in bad ways. In that sense, he forms part of our mind or consciousness – a far cry from the resoundingly terrifying creature employed through the ages to strike fear into us and to keep us in check.

Come to think of it, though, we would want to be careful in casually dismissing the devil as a grotesque physical being. At least that is according to an entertaining and amusing insight provided by the nineteenth-century French poet, essayist and critic Charles Baudelaire. Writing of an imaginary encounter with Lucifer in *The Generous Gambler*, he described how 'His Highness' said that he feared his game was up when he heard a preacher telling his flock that 'the devil's best trick is to persuade you that he doesn't exist.' Perhaps the preacher was right – you can never trust Lucifer, the crafty old goat!

PURGATORY

O n 31 October 1517, an ordinary-looking monk, of
thin frame and average height, walked up to the front
door of the church in Wittenberg, Germany. There was
nothing exceptional about the monk's demeanour. Aged 33,
dressed in his friar's robes and with a tonsured head, he looked
like any other monk one might see.

The monk nailed a copy of a piece of paper to the door. He
had been carrying it in his hand all the way from the friary at
the edge of town. Although seemingly innocuous, the document
– *The Ninety-Five Theses* – had the impact of a major nuclear
explosion, ripping apart the foundations of the Roman Catholic
Church and starting what would eventually be known as the
Protestant Reformation.

There were two simple words at the core of Martin Luther's
incendiary document: purgatory and indulgences. The first of those
words – purgatory – refers to the place where souls supposedly
go to for punishment and cleansing before moving on to heaven.
The second word – indulgences – refers to remissions granted
towards that punishment, thus lessening its duration. The two
words were proving to be very bad company for each other at
the time.

Luther had chosen his moment well. The following day – All
Saints' Day – hundreds of pilgrims would be arriving to view
the church's collection of relics. They consisted of 19,000 bones
and 5,000 other objects, many of them highly dubious – such

as a supposed strand of hair from the beard of Jesus, some purported bread from the Last Supper, and a most unlikely portion of straw from Christ's manger. To secure the remissions on offer, you queued and paid with cash.

The notion that you could buy your way out of purgatory sickened Luther. So did a lot of other things going on in the church at the time. Saints' images and relics were being hawked around Europe to raise church funds, based on fraudulent claims that they could bring about miraculous cures. Cinders masquerading as those from the blaze that roasted St. Lawrence were being brought from one village to the next to raise money.

So wide was the proliferation of 'true' pieces of the cross that the Catholic theologian Erasmus contended that a substantial ship could be made from them if they were collected together in one great pile. Nails said to be from the cross were flooding the continent. Fourteen European churches claimed to have in their possession the head of John the Baptist.

Things were just as bad on the indulgences front. From the fourteenth century onwards, the number of indulgences had spiralled. Many churches offered them in return for monetary contributions and attending mass, with 40 days being granted by one church for turning up to a particular service. Monks journeyed far and wide selling them to raise money for their monasteries. Plenary indulgences – granting total remission of sin – were offered to those who provided one per cent of their income or possessions to support one of the Crusades.

The entire racket had spiralled out of control. Tables were drawn up linking the amount to be paid with the punishment to be remitted. Indulgences were sold to murderers and rapists as ways to escape guilt and punishment. One unscrupulous Dominican, named Tetzel, was said to have proclaimed: 'Even if you have deflowered the Virgin Mary, an indulgence will free you from punishment in purgatory!'

Things became so bad that, in 1521, a Dutch pamphlet appeared with the title *A devout book for everyone who wants to go to heaven without passing through purgatory*, with a total of 224,000 years of indulgences included in its pages. A famous Dutch rhyme summed up the shoddy trade: 'When a penny rings in the collection box, a soul from purgatory is freed.' Unsurprisingly, Erasmus was prompted to write to a friend: 'What is there more shameless than these endless indulgences?'

This corrupt scheme of purgatory and indulgences found its origins in a suggestion made more than two millennia earlier indicating that there might be a destination where our souls are cleansed before being admitted to paradise. The suggestion came from the prophet Zechariah. Writing five centuries before Christ, he hinted that while some souls went directly to life everlasting and others straight to hell, there were more who would be dealt with in an in-between way.

'This third I will put into the fire,' Zechariah quotes God as saying. 'I will refine them like silver and test them like gold. They will call on my name and I will answer them.' The inference seemed to be that those in this 'third' category – most likely the almost good but not totally bad – could achieve purification and atone for their sins.

Another text – Maccabees, which was also written before Christ – seemed to likewise imply the existence of some sort of post-death, in-between state. We are told how, after Judas Maccabeus and members of his army collected bodies of comrades who had fallen in battle, they prayed for the dead that they might be forgiven their sins. People asked why such prayers would be necessary if the only afterlife alternatives were a heaven and a hell! What use would the prayers be otherwise?

The issue of how the prayers of the living could influence the destinies of the dead surfaced again in the sixth century. This time it arose in the writings of the powerful Church luminary Pope Gregory I. Those who read what he wrote – and many did – must have been surprised and relieved by his declaration that some 'little and very small sins' may be cleansed in the next world. He included among those sins 'daily idle talk, immoderate laughter, negligence in the care of our family' and 'ignorant errors in matters of no great weight.'

Pope Gregory I claimed that prayers could help these hapless souls. Writing in his immensely-popular book *Dialogues*, which was put together in the late sixth century, he featured stories illustrating his point of view. One of them concerned 'a certain man' whose spirit appeared to the pastor of the church of St. John in the Italian city of Tauriana. The spirit appeared in real-life form, working as a lowly attendant at the local hot-water baths.

One day, on being offered 'holy bread' by the priest, the man declined, saying he had died and had been sent to do this menial job as punishment for his sins. 'I cannot eat of it,' the man said, 'but if you desire to pleasure me, offer this bread unto almighty God, and be an intercessor for my sins; and by this shall you know that your prayers be heard, if at your next coming you find me not here.' He then vanished out of sight. After a week of offering masses for the man's soul, the priest returned to the baths and 'found him not there.'

Behind Pope Gregory's expositions lay an issue of widespread public debate and Church concern at that time. The issue was this – some people might be good enough to go directly to heaven; others might be sufficiently evil to go straight to hell, but the majority will fall somewhere in the middle. Finding it hard to accept that lesser wrongdoings would lead to eternal damnation, the faithful hoped that there must be another place of punishment where transgressors could atone for their sins and prepare for heaven.

An important feature of the debate was what manner of punishment might be meted out in this in-between place and for how long it might last. The nature and intensity of the suffering was understood to vary widely, with accounts and interpretations describing anything from extreme torture to mental anguish. Some accounts identified physical burnings similar to the fires of hell; others suggested 'inner fires' where the mind is tortured for past wrongdoings and failings.

It was sometimes proposed that the suffering could not be physical as, after death, the body no longer exists and only the soul enters into purgatory. Others counter-proposed that, if God wishes, then the suffering could feel of a physical nature even if a body is no longer there. More suggested that both these propositions miss the point – the absence from the goodness of God, no matter how temporary, is all that matters and is punishment enough.

A slightly different take on these propositions is well worth mentioning. This thesis proposed that purgatory is the state where we assess and analyse our former sins, misdeeds and wrongdoings, recall our failings and acts of unkindness, and evaluate the hurtful and unsavoury behaviour of our past lives. It is only when we have addressed these transgressions and are sorry for them that we will qualify to progress to everlasting happiness. This particular proposition, which is similar to what people who have had near-death experiences report, will be of special interest in the next, and final, chapter of this book.

The idea that prayerful intercession benefits the souls of the dead gathered momentum around the turn of the first millennium when Odilo, the Benedictine Abbot of Cluny, set aside a special day of prayer which he called All Souls' Day and instructed that it be celebrated on 2 November. The idea soon spread from Cluny to other monasteries, and from there spread throughout the Western Church.

The story behind All Souls' Day is interesting and worth noting. Legend has it that a monk who was returning to Europe from Jerusalem was shipwrecked in a storm. His boat was driven onto an island or rock. There he met a hermit who, having learned that the monk knew Odilo of Cluny, asked him to pass on a message.

The message revealed that near the hermit's refuge was a place where great fires belched forth and into which tortured sinners were thrust. A multitude of demons received them and inflicted torments and unbearable sufferings. The hermit often heard the demons complain that through the prayers and alms-givings of monks – especially the monks of Cluny – many of the damned went free.

The hermit implored Odilo and his monks to intensify their prayers. They would thereby 'cause the angels to rejoice and the devil to rage,' was how L. M. Smith described the expected impact in her century-old book *The Early History of the Monastery of Cluny*. As a result, Odilo instituted his special day of intercession for the souls of the dead and instructed his monks to say private prayers and public masses for the faithful dead. So began All Souls' Day, which was first held in the year 998 and has persisted ever since.

It wasn't until the twelfth and thirteenth centuries – around three or four centuries before Luther's famous outburst – that the fever surrounding purgatory intensified and the concept really took off. A papal letter from 1253 signalled its first official acceptance by the Catholic Church, which later defined it and established it as church doctrine.

Interest in this neither-here-nor-there realm quickly gained momentum. Churchmen loved it, recognising its potential for instilling fear in the faithful and for strengthening control over their flocks. Prayers for the dead were promoted. Mary became known as the 'Queen of Purgatory', a great intercessor. As we saw, purgatory also had the not incidental effect of generating lots of revenue on the side.

Like all newly-popular ideas, purgatory's tentacles spread far and wide – into books, art, poetry, conversation and religious dogma. Its spread was helped by developments in printing, init-ially by the replacement of hand-copying with wooden block reproduction techniques and, later, by the introduction of the printing press.

Written expositions of purgatory became prolific. From the twelfth century onwards, one account after the other appeared, with each outdoing the previous one in their descriptions of purgatory. Some clearly copied the style and content of those that had preceded them; many set out to score points and deliver preordained messages.

One of the best known of these twelfth-century accounts concerned the Irishman named Tundale who we read about in the previous chapter. The soul of this nobleman and knight was said to have embarked on a voyage to the other side after he collapsed and was believed to have died. Accompanied by an angel, he was brought on a tour of the afterlife, including a place where he witnessed 'the moderate pain of the not-very-bad.' His story became hugely popular throughout Europe and elsewhere.

'They saw a very high wall, and within the wall on the side they were coming from they saw a great multitude of men and women enduring wind and rain,' the Tundale account revealed, describing purgatorial punishment that was mild compared to the horrific torments of the damned. 'They were very sad, enduring hunger and thirst; nevertheless they had light and did not smell the stench.

'The soul asked, "Who are these who linger in a place like this?" The angel responded, "These souls are evil, but not very evil. Indeed they tried to follow honestly, but in good times they were not generous to the poor, as they should have been, and therefore for many years they deserve to suffer this rain: then they will be led to a good place."'

Another of these vision expositions rose to prominence in the early thirteenth century. The account concerned that humble man from London, Thurkill, who we heard from earlier in this book. He saw penitent souls awaiting prayers so they might gain entry to a temple where 'the spirits of the just, whiter than snow' were living. The more special the prayer offerings they received, the closer they came to the church, Thurkill remarked.

A third graphic description of purgatorial torments resulted from a twelfth-century visit to St. Patrick's Purgatory in Ireland's Lough Derg. Situated in a landscape of bogs and forests, this tiny island in County Donegal became internationally famous for its cave which was purported to be an entryway to purgatory. Many noteworthy people of the era entered the dark, narrow structure and emerged with horrific descriptions of 'sights hidden from mortal eye.'

The legendary visit in 1153 – at the time when purgatory was first coming to prominence – was undertaken by a knight named Owen. Consumed by guilt over the wicked life he had led, he travelled to St. Patrick's Purgatory where the punishments he witnessed were gruesome – fiery dragons gnawing at sinners with metallic teeth, serpents digging fangs into sinners' hearts, some sinners being immersed in cauldrons full of liquid pitch, others being suspended over fires of brimstone by iron chains.

These dreadful torments, he was informed, were the sufferings undertaken for sins committed in life. Having completed their punishments, the purified souls then entered a place of rest prior to their elevation to heaven – a wondrous place, he said, containing 'the most delightful meadows, adorned with different flowers and fruits of many kinds of herbs and trees.' He felt he could survive forever on their sweet odours.

Although the images described by the Knight Owen were mixed – ranging from horrific tortures to a tranquil waiting room – it was the gruesome, hideous punishments of purgatory that left their mark. Simple, poor, uneducated churchgoers were terrified. Their fears were intensified by the famines, plagues and prolonged wars that would soon take place, generating further interest in what awaited them after death.

These spine-chilling physical punishments represented only part of the picture. There also was the inner turmoil of those condemned to purgatory – the acute guilt over sin, the intense remorse, self-reproach, feelings of unworthiness and anguish at being excluded from the presence of God. The sixteenth-century Spanish mystic and saint, Teresa of Ávila, described this type of punishment well.

'The pain of loss, or the privation of the sight of God, exceeds all the most excruciating sufferings we can imagine,' St. Teresa wrote. 'Picture to yourself a shipwrecked mariner who, after having long battled with the waves, comes at last within reach of the shore, only to find himself constantly thrust back by an invisible hand. What torturing agonies! Yet those of the souls in purgatory are a thousand times greater.'

This feeling of loss was also articulated in a story recounted by another Spanish mystic, Juan Eusebio Nieremberg, a Jesuit who was born in Madrid in 1595 to German parents. He described a case said to have occurred in Treves, where a deceased woman appeared to a young girl. The woman requested that three masses might be offered on her behalf. This the young girl did.

Year after year, the woman appeared and, each time, was clearly still in exile. On one occasion, she revealed that she had suffered 'the pain of loss' and 'the privation of God.' This privation, she said, 'caused her intolerable torture.' Eventually, she 'thanked the pious girl for her prayers, and rose to heaven in company with her guardian angel.'

How long this woman's soul languished in purgatory is unknown. Exactly how much time is meant to be attached to each sin is unknown, too. However, a study of the literature is both interesting and revealing. Some relevant references exist, although they are often buried in obscure texts, with most of the sources stretching back hundreds of years; some even extending as far back as the early years of the second millennium.

In one report, from 1859, a deceased soul appeared stating that it had already been 77 full years in purgatory. In another account, dating from the late fourteenth to the early fifteenth century, a Dominican friar's deceased sister appeared stating that she had been condemned to undergo torments 'until the day of the last judgement.'

A further account – this time dating from 1917 – derived from a well-reported appearance by Our Lady to three young children at Fatima, Portugal. On Sunday, 13 May 1917, the children were heading for home after tending sheep and playing when Our Lady was said to appear 'all dressed in white, more brilliant than the sun.' The children stopped and a conversation ensued.

Some of the questions asked by Lucia – one of the three young children – concerned the afterlife fates of two friends who had recently died. 'Is Maria das Neves already in heaven?' she queried. Our Lady answered, 'Yes, she is.' 'And Amelia?' Lucy also asked. 'She will be in purgatory until the end of the world,' the apparition responded, indicating a less than desirable outcome for this girl described as being 'between 18 and 20 years old.'

Yet another lost soul – that of Pope Innocent III, who died in 1216 – is reputed to have described punishments stretching ahead of him for hundreds of years. The broad spectrum of durations led the Italian Jesuit, Cardinal Robert Bellarmine, to conclude: 'There is no doubt that the pains of purgatory are not limited to ten or 20 years, and that they last in some cases entire centuries.'

As we might expect, the duration of punishment was said to depend on the nature and extent of the sins; and the number of sins certainly mattered. The seventeenth-century Jesuit, Fr. James Mumford, took a stab at the figures. Suppose, he said, you commit ten faults a day. That amounts to 3,650 faults a year. Round off that figure to 3,000 and at the end of 20 years you have accumulated 60,000 faults.

Let us presume, he added, that one-half of these faults are wiped clean by penance and good works. That leaves 30,000 faults to be atoned for. Perhaps, he said, it is reasonable to suppose that each fault gets one hour in purgatory, although he stressed that 'this measure is very moderate.' You are left with 30,000 hours of punishment in purgatory.

With relentless logic, he went on to propose that if you allow for a day per fault instead of just one hour, then you are in deep trouble. If you add in mortal sins – punishable by seven years for each mortal sin, according to St. Frances of Rome – then you are in deeper trouble still. He concluded that you may arrive before God with a sentence facing you of 'an appalling duration,' lasting perhaps for centuries.

The nature of time in purgatory posed a further dilemma. Does one hour on earth, or one year on earth, equate with the same length of time in the realm of temporary punishment? Could it be that, whatever the length of time, the sheer intensity of the torments makes it feel even longer? This, again, has been dealt with in the form of a purportedly true story.

The tale – recounted by the fifteenth-century Dominican St. Antoninus – recalls the case of a seriously-ill monk who had been unwell for some time. His pain was so severe that he pleaded with God to let him die. One day, his guardian angel came to him with a proposition. 'You have two choices,' the angel said. 'You can continue to suffer for a year and then die and go straight to heaven. Alternatively, you can die now and go to purgatory, where you will be punished for three days.'

The decision seemed an easy one for the long-suffering monk – he chose the three days of punishment in purgatory. After one hour, he was visited by the guardian angel. 'Why have you left me here to suffer these torments?' he demanded to know. 'You promised me I would only be here for three days.' The guardian angel asked: 'How long do you think you have been here?' He replied: 'For several years.' Having been told that he had only been there for one hour, he concluded that an hour in purgatory is probably the equivalent of six years of torment on earth.

Within five decades of the printing of the story you have just read, the concept of purgatory, and the indulgences associated with it, had been blown out of the water by Martin Luther's *The Ninety-Five Theses*. An enormous schism within Western Christianity ensued. To this day, none of the major Protestant faiths express belief in an intermediate purgatorial state between heaven and hell, regarding it as unbiblical. They also reject the validity of indulgences.

The Catholic Church, too, changed its position in the wake of the Protestant Reformation. In 1563, the Council of Trent condemned 'all base gain for securing indulgences' and, four years later, the sale of indulgences was brought to an end by Pope Pius V. Despite these developments, both purgatory and indulgences retain their place within Catholicism.

For Catholics, purgatory continues to be recognised as a transitory state of purification, while indulgences continue to act as a type of amnesty against the sanctions to be endured. Prayers are still said to help the souls of the dead, both individually and collectively. Yet the crass monetary exploitation of the link between purgatory and indulgences is gone.

For believers in Islam, there was no need for any change in the status of purgatory as the concept was never recognised in the first place. The alternatives facing those who die are either Paradise or damnation. This latter option is both horrible and eternal, unless willed otherwise by God.

This get-out clause regarding the will of God is interesting to note and does have significance. It is believed that at judgement day by God's will certain sinners will be released from hell and transferred to Paradise. To the extent that this implies that these sinners will only suffer temporary punishments, it is vaguely similar to purgatory. Beyond that, the concept of purgatory is alien to Islam.

It is also interesting – indeed, curious – to note that not one of my temporary-death interviewees has ever made reference to purgatory. They have spoken about the wonders of heaven and the horrors of hell but they never identified purgatory with its prolonged, but limited, punishments for sinners. This seems odd as they recall their heavenly and hellish encounters with vivid intensity and clarity, marking them out as highpoints of their travels. One might expect the same of purgatory if it exists.

This omission is particularly strange when you consider that every other element of the near-death experience – the departure from the body, the light, the feelings of peace, the judgement and the experiencing of God and love – feature prominently in almost all ancient sacred texts. Perhaps the difficulty in finding anything but the vaguest references to purgatory in these documents arises because it is not something that features after death.

There is an alternative explanation – namely, that the assessing of past misdemeanours which people say they experience during the judgement phase of the near-death experience, and the feelings of remorse and concern that are often felt at that time, may constitute the phenomenon of purgatory. Perhaps, then, the evaluating of one's life's deeds during this process, and the associated worry over whether heaven will be the person's final destination, is what this germ of an idea called purgatory describes. Should that be so, then purgatory is clearly an infinitely more attractive proposition than hell which, as we saw, is a lot more fearsome indeed.

YOU CANNOT DIE

Elsie suffered a near-fatal brain haemorrhage in 2005. It started with a strange buzzing in her ear. Her symptoms intensified, resulting in her being rushed by ambulance to hospital. The prospects were grim. Her doctor predicted she wouldn't last the journey; following her arrival, hospital staff told her family she wouldn't survive.

At some stage, Elsie, who was then in her early 60s, departed her body and reached the borders of death. She entered a tunnel and travelled to a world of love and light. It wasn't any particular place, she told me, just somewhere indescribably special, a place she knew to be the home of God.

'I was enveloped in love,' Elsie recalled of her journey that day. 'I can't explain the feeling of love; it was so unreal, so not belonging to this world. There was light there, as well; light and heat and warmth. The light was bright, yet it didn't hurt my eyes. But the love I felt....oh, my goodness! I will never forget it. It was the sort of love that you can't get from a human being or a human bond. It was out of this world.

'I thought about where I was going, who I was going to meet and what I was going to be doing. I felt, "This is it! I have been studying all my life to be in this great position. I am now reaching the ultimate in what I always wanted to be and what I was always looking for." I felt it was a completion. There was an expectation of greatness. It's what I had prepared for.

'Everything I was feeling was what I would have expected from God. I felt I was in his presence. I had knowledge within me that I was going to meet him. I was getting closer all the time. I had just about reached him when I stopped. A voice very clearly said to me, "Be still and know that I am God! I am the Lord that's healing thee!"

'I then started to come back. As I did so, I knew I wouldn't have been able to survive for much longer in that love. It was so intense. It was so overpowering. I was then back in my body, in the hospital.'

This compelling story raises an important question – what exactly was Elsie experiencing at the time of her temporary death? The answer is clear – hers was a near-death experience. Most of the main elements were there – departure from the body, tunnel travel, the bright light that didn't hurt her eyes, the profound sense of love, a feeling of being in the presence of God, an intense desire to reach her destination, and the eventual return to her body.

As near-death experiences go, Elsie's story is a classic example of what people – young and old, male and female, believers and non-believers – have reported in all corners of the globe, at all times throughout recorded history. The sheer volume of cases and the consistency of the details recalled are convincing. It has led many eminent researchers – including those who conducted a four-year University of Southampton study involving more than 2,000 cardiac-arrest patients, published in 2014 – to conclude that life does indeed continue after clinical death.

What happens after we die requires close analysis, and I will begin by examining 'the light'. Those who experience near-death say that after we pass away we perceive an intense light ahead, drawing us to it. Its radiance surrounds us and bathes us in its warmth. It enables us to see the wonders of where we are going. Without it, there would be darkness. With it, we can observe with a sort of clarity unknown to us in life.

The light, they say, allows us to see much more than physical objects. We comprehend and perceive like we never did before. We become enlightened. We understand everything, including the greatness of God and his universe. Because of its relationship to awareness, this light is often said to be our consciousness, or sometimes our spirit or our soul.

Ancient mystics understood the light to be at the core of creation, prompting them to declare 'God is light.' The world of science has also underscored the primacy of light, with physicist Stephen Hawking proclaiming that subatomic particles, broken down, are 'nothing but pure light.' In short, light is at the root of everything. What happens to our own personal light – our consciousness, as I will call it from now on – is the challenge facing us ahead.

The central issue is straightforward. If our consciousness is produced by the brain then surely it dies when the brain dies. On the other hand, if it can be shown to originate from elsewhere then it is likely that it can survive the process of dying. The key is the nature and origin of consciousness. Establish that it exists independently and we have found gold dust in our search for an afterlife in the light.

Welcome to the weird and wonderful world of quantum mechanics – a frustratingly complicated area of scientific investigation which can be as baffling to experts as to ordinary laymen. A realm of subatomic particles, parallel universes and alternate realities, it is an investigative field that has both challenged and undermined man's age-old understanding of science and, in doing so, raised questions about the meaning of reality and nature's deepest designs.

Quantum mechanics has been a source of great surprises, especially when it comes to the issue of life after death. It has raised the prospect of consciousness survival, of other worlds we may live in after we die, of the meaninglessness of death itself. As Professor Robert Lanza – an expert in the field and one of the world's leading scientists – concluded: 'Death does not exist in any real sense.' Clearly, when an authority such as this makes a remark like that, we need to carefully consider what quantum mechanics has to offer in our search for clues to the afterlife.

The truth is that quantum mechanics not only has a lot to say, but many of its studies have largely confirmed what we have known for millennia – that a plausible case exists that we do live on after death. A number of these investigations have concluded that, unlike our bodies which physically decay, our consciousness or soul survives elsewhere. This conclusion, of course, would also pertain to animals as they too exhibit consciousness in their lives.

One theory proposes that our brains are antennae that tap into a universal consciousness which exists all around us. We are, in other words, just like TV antennae, picking up external signals and information. Should this be so, then our external consciousness, or soul, doesn't die with us but lives on after death – thereby confirming one of the fundamental tenets of the world's main religions. The theory also validates the remarkably-prescient views on cosmic, or universal, consciousness of Eastern faiths.

A version of this proposition has been put forward by the American author and academic, Dr. Paul L. Nunez, who presents the case in his book *Brain, Mind, and the Structure of Reality*. He argues that consciousness might well be an information field separate from our bodies that is detected and tapped into by brain tissue. This viewpoint, he says, while seeming preposterous in the context of classical scientific thinking, 'appears much more credible when viewed in the context of modern physical theories.'

Nunez's theory – culled from the world of quantum mechanics – opens up the possibility of afterlife survival. Once the heart stops beating and the brain flatlines, the physical body begins the process of entropy and decay. Our consciousness, on the other hand, lives on. Apart from substantiating the proposition of life after death, his theory also helps explain why so many people claim to feel the continuing presence of loved ones after they die; although physically dead, their consciousness lives on and can be sensed.

Another theory argues that information in our brains leaves us after we die and enters the universe at large. There it continues to exist, not unlike the way many religions believe our soul exits the body and survives after death. This proposition has been put forward by the eminent British mathematician Sir Roger Penrose, who is Professor of Mathematics at Oxford University, and Dr. Stuart Hameroff, who is Professor of Anaesthesiology at the University of Arizona.

These experts argue that the essence of what we refer to as our soul is to be found in structures called microtubules which exist within our brain cells. The microtubules contain brain information. When we die, this information – which constitutes our consciousness or soul – doesn't die with us but travels back into the universe.

The theory confirms the belief commonly shared by world religions that the soul departs the body on death and survives somewhere else, in a heaven or paradise. It also explains the near-death experience, where the soul or consciousness leaves the body but eventually returns.

'Let's say the heart stops beating, the blood stops flowing,' Dr. Hameroff explains regarding the near-death experience. 'The quantum information within the microtubules is not destroyed, it can't be destroyed, it just distributes and dissipates to the universe at large. If the patient is resuscitated, revived, this quantum information can go back into the microtubules and the patient says, "I had a near-death experience."'

On the other hand, if the person doesn't survive, the information may not necessarily linger forever in the universe at large. Instead, it may enter the brain cells of someone else, perhaps a newborn child – in other words, it is reincarnated or reborn. In this way, the theory also accounts for the reincarnation and rebirth beliefs of Hinduism, Buddhism and early Christianity outlined in this book.

It can also be said that the theory implies that, once we die, we will join those who have predeceased us and live on in the same time-space together – substantiating yet another told-you-so of many world faiths. Although the work of Penrose and Hameroff has generated scientific controversy and debate, subsequent research findings have validated their proposition.

Quantum mechanics has gone even further than the theories of consciousness just outlined and has provided us with a range of alternative worlds we might survive in after death. This is strange territory, indeed – a place of multiple universes where our souls might progress to, and live on in, after we die. It is a complex field of investigation, but it is worth examining in our afterlife quest.

One of the most prominent and influential investigators in this field was the brilliant American physicist and mathematician Hugh Everett III. Reduced to its simplest level, his 1957 theory proposed that a countless number of universes exist, with our universe being just one of them. Each universe keeps expanding, just like the branches of a tree, into entirely separate but parallel worlds.

The outcomes of our lives differ in each of these universes. In one, we might die in a traffic accident; in another, we might survive it. In one, we might die aged 67; in another, death might come at 93. For the Everett family, there was a sad footnote to the father's innovative work – in 1996, 14 years after Everett's death, his daughter committed suicide leaving a note saying she hoped to end up in the same parallel universe as her father.

An additional refinement of the concept of multiple universes was put forward by Professor Robert Lanza, who we briefly heard from earlier in this chapter. Not only is he one of the world's leading scientists, as mentioned earlier, but he was voted by *Time* magazine in 2014 as one of the '100 Most Influential People in the World.' His theory proposes that life continues after the body dies. Life can also last forever.

Lanza's basic idea is simple – when we die we end up in a world similar to the one we once lived in, but we are again alive. This process continues to infinity, whereby we move from one world to another, leading Professor Lanza to his conclusion mentioned earlier that 'death does not exist in any real sense.' Instead, he says, our life is like a 'perennial flower that returns to bloom in the multiverse.'

The notion that consciousness survives outside the physical body – whether or not in the manner outlined so far – is, of course, an old one. Plato had already tackled the issue four centuries before Christ, arguing that the soul was a nonmaterial entity with an independent existence separate from the body. The seventeenth-century philosopher René Descartes proposed a broadly similar view. Although the advent of modern-day quantum mechanics has brought startling new perspectives, traditional classical science has had much to offer, too.

The theory underlying the premise that we survive physical death was first formulated in the fifth century before Christ. It came from the outstanding brain of the philosopher and poet Empedocles, who was born into a wealthy, noble family and whose grandfather was the horse race champion at the Olympic Games in 496 BC. A colourful character, known for wearing purple robes, fine sandals and a wreath of laurels, he made a groundbreaking contribution to what would one day become a fundamental law of physics.

Empedocles proposed that four basic elements – earth, air, fire and water – were at the root of all things animate and inanimate. Different combinations of the four elements resulted in the creation of different things including people. He called these elements 'roots', broadly anticipating the scientific identification of atoms more than 2,000 years later. Due to his extraordinary revelations, Empedocles was revered by his fellow Greeks as someone akin to a living god.

The implications of Empedocles' remarkable investigations were immense. Everything originates from the four basic elements; in other words, nothing comes from nothing. Likewise, nothing can be destroyed into nothing; instead, things reduce to their constituent elements. The inference was clear – a human being doesn't die and decay into nothing; instead, the elements that made it exist in the first place live on.

Empedocles' idea that the fundamental elements in all things are indestructible and everlasting formed the basis of scientific belief for the next 2,000 years. Eventually, carefully conducted scientific experiments showed that his theory had been right from the start. Many of these investigations were conducted by a similarly dashing and wealthy intellectual, Antoine Lavoisier, a Parisian nobleman who became known as the 'Father of Modern Chemistry'.

Before Lavoisier's famous experiments, conducted in the eighteenth century, some people had doubted the principle of conservation of mass. Weigh a piece of wood, burn it, and then weigh it again – and, without fail, the weight of the ashes will be less than the original weight of the wood. 'Principle disproved!' sceptics proclaimed. Unknown to those sceptics, however, the cause was that gases had escaped into the air.

The methodical chemist Lavoisier was ahead of the game and used sealed glass vessels to conduct similar tests, ensuring that gases couldn't escape measurement. He conducted test after test, including tests involving the burning of wood, and at the end of each the weight was the same as it was at the beginning. Nothing, according to his law of conservation of mass, ever disappears but is only transformed. To put it another way, everything lives on but in a different form.

The implication from Lavoisier's work was not lost on those who wondered whether we live on after death. The laws of matter govern all aspects of the universe – animate and inanimate – including the physical body. Our bodies might seemingly

194

disappear following death, but the matter underlying them cannot. There can be no extinction and, in that sense, no end of life.

The debate became even more intriguing for those interested in survival after death when the scientific community turned its attention from matter to energy. We all understand the concept of energy – the power, force, vigour or zeal that drives us and keeps us going. It's what seemingly distinguishes us from a rock, which is lifeless, immobile and stationary. Our personal energy might be described – as the late seventeenth- and early eighteenth-century philosopher Gottfried Leibniz put it – as our 'life force' or 'living force.' As others put it, it might be said to constitute our soul.

It's really to Leibniz that we owe gratitude for discovering the first formal scientific connection between matter and energy. Without going into the complicated details – and the scientific definition of energy *is* complicated – suffice to say that the results of his investigation, and all the investigations that followed, established a definitive connection between matter and energy and showed, in effect, that energy is an intrinsic property of all objects.

These investigations concluded that, just like matter, energy can be converted into different forms but it cannot be created or destroyed. The eminent theoretical physicist and Nobel Prize winner, Albert Einstein, articulated the point succinctly: 'Energy cannot be created or destroyed; it can only be changed from one form to another.' For those who wondered about the energy – or life force, or living force, or soul – departing from a body on death, what he said was fascinating, indeed.

The possible connection between loss of energy and departure of the soul is readily apparent from our everyday lives. At one time or another, we must have all noticed how, once a person dies, the body becomes drained and immobile, devoid of energy and effervescence. What leaves the body, it might be said, is that energising force that once gave it exuberance and life. The ancient Greeks put it simply – after death a person is no longer 'ensouled' or, to employ the word they used, is no longer 'alive'.

We might wonder, then, if this loss of energy or mass – this departure of the soul – can be physically identified and measured. Regarding identification, many who experience death say they have sensed something ineffable and immaterial leaving the body around the time it expires. One woman who had a near-death experience described to me how she felt her 'other self' departing from her body through the back of her head. 'It was like something had come up through my body, gone out through my head and was gone,' she said.

Another interviewee – who likewise experienced near-death – felt her soul draining away through the mattress. She said: 'I could feel my whole being, from the top of my head to my toes, being sucked out of me down through the mattress. It was like everything was draining out of me, a bit like how water might soak out of the bottom of a wet sponge. It wasn't painful or anything. It just happened and I was gone.'

There really is nothing new or extraordinary in these graphic revelations. Throughout history, similar accounts have been recorded, dating back to the early Egyptians whose hieroglyphics showed bird-like souls departing from the body at the time of death. The soul of the Irish saint Laisrén was said to have exited from his body through the crown of his head. Medieval accounts frequently stated that the soul left by the mouth.

Given these historical and modern-day observations, it is reasonable to conjecture that the process might – and I stress 'might' – be open to scientific measurement. Consider the basic principle again – nothing ever disappears but is only transformed. By deduction, some weight loss might be expected to follow the soul's exit from the body. You will note I used the word 'might' again as the proposition is based on the premise that the soul has mass and is not just information as was postulated earlier in this chapter.

Dr. Duncan MacDougall, a respected American physician from Massachusetts, tackled this issue in 1901. He postulated that if a soul leaves the body on death then it must have occupied space in the body before death occurred. Continuing with his reasoning, he concluded that anything that occupies space must have weight. His task, then, was to weigh bodies at the point of death. Any loss of weight would indicate the departure of something, perhaps the soul.

His initial experiment – conducted using a male dying from consumption – was undertaken on 10 April, 1901. The result was interesting. At the precise point of death, a weight loss of three-quarters of an ounce was recorded. Although he conducted five similar experiments, using five other patients, with varying results, his three-quarters of an ounce conclusion from the first experiment is often referred to even today. It became, when converted into grams, the title of the 2003 movie, *21 Grams*, starring Sean Penn.

Another investigator, Harry La Verne Twining, undertook similar experiments in the early 1900s, but this time involving animals. Using mice and cats, he claimed to have shown that weight loss was experienced at the time of their deaths. The conclusion drawn, in this case, was that animals – just like humans – have souls that survive physical extinction.

Twining later dismissed his experiments, pointing out that moisture loss was most likely the cause of the fall in weight – a conclusion that might equally apply to MacDougall's experiments involving humans. In either case, the experiments may well have been facile as consciousness or soul – as we have seen in recent quantum investigations – is likely to be weightless.

In retrospect, the idea of measuring the weight of the soul – although novel – was little more than a curious footnote in the history of afterlife research. Conducted over a century ago, the experiments seem ponderous and outdated compared to the mind-blowing insights which quantum mechanics presents to us today. This is especially true regarding consciousness and the role it plays in determining the reality of our existence and our survival after death.

Modern science has some fascinating things to say about consciousness. We have already seen how it may be external to us, floating around in the universe at large – in a place religions often refer to as heaven or paradise or some other afterlife destination. What we haven't discussed is the power of this mysterious entity and the role it plays in our lives.

Consciousness is different from the brain. While the brain is like a computer, controlling functions and movements, among many other things, we must look elsewhere to explain our self-awareness and awareness of the world that surrounds us, our feelings, personality traits, thoughts and beliefs, and our ability to create or choose. These, according to the English philosopher, Gilbert Ryle, are the 'Ghost in the Machine', the elusive, indefinable entity many refer to as our soul.

This soul, or consciousness, not only defines who we are but may even create the reality that surrounds us. This was illustrated in one of the most extraordinary investigations ever undertaken – the double-slit experiment. Although it started out as a fairly straightforward scientific test, it soon had scientists scratching their heads in disbelief.

The experiment was simple enough. A series of photons, or light particles, was fired at a barrier with two slits. A plate was set up behind the barrier, marking which slit each photon had passed through. When observed, the photons behaved in a predictable and logical way – they went through either one slit or the other.

What was truly mind-blowing, however, was that when the experiment wasn't observed, the marks on the plate behind the barrier showed that the photons behaved differently. Instead of acting individually and passing through either of the slits, they behaved like waves and *passed through both slits at the same time*.

This outcome was eye-opening, to say the least, even quite staggering. How could it be that when photons are observed they behave like individual particles, whereas they transform into waves when not being watched? Could they be capable of deception, just like children changing their behaviour within sight of their parents? Interesting though this explanation may appear to be, it falls wide of the mark.

The truth, it seems, may be more startling. Those photons, when observed, behaved as they did because our consciousness determined that they should do so. It's our consciousness that created the reality. It's the same with all things – physical reality doesn't exist; it is we who create it. Perhaps John Lennon expressed this principle well when he wrote that 'nothing is real' in 'Strawberry Fields Forever' – nothing is intrinsically real; it's only we who create it.

In the same way, it is we who define our lives and mark out our personal reality. We determine what we are – cruel or kind, polite or rude, honest or deceitful, generous or mean-spirited. Our mind – or our consciousness, as we might call it – determines which of these apply to us. As the Buddha said, 'All that we are is the result of what we have thought. The mind is everything. What we think, we become.'

Presuming that our mind or consciousness survives death, the inferences for a good or bad afterlife are clear. After physical death, everything that our mind represents – including our darkest secrets, guilt, anger and resentments – lives on. Presuming that these issues are unresolved – among them, heartless and dishonest behaviour or a legacy of pain and wrongs inflicted on others – then the prospects of experiencing a troubled afterlife can be said to be high.

The near-death experience bears this out. Take, for example, a woman I interviewed who experienced near-death immediately after the birth of her daughter. No sooner was the baby delivered than she departed her body, travelled through a tunnel and headed for the light. Almost instantly, she felt fear and terror, including a crystal-clear understanding that she didn't merit an afterlife in heaven.

'I had this awful fear and terror of what was going to happen to me,' she told me. 'I'm sure part of it was because of guilt over my mother. I had prayed and cried in despair, for four years, because of my relationship with her....My problem was guilt....I felt like an Antichrist. I was ashamed of my feelings....I suppose I thought I was going to hell.'

The woman informed me of what it felt like going through the tunnel. It didn't feel like she was in her body, she explained, it was more like her '*consciousness* going through.' Like many others who undergo near-death, what she described – and the term she used – was uncannily similar to what we now read in the studies and investigations from the world of quantum mechanics.

Those who are in a positive state prior to death tell a very different story. One woman who had temporarily died having haemorrhaged following a miscarriage described to me how she experienced a pleasant journey before eventually returning to her body. As she pointed out, 'There was nothing in my life I was ashamed of or guilty about.' Today, when a person is dying, she envies 'the beautiful experience that is awaiting them.'

Judgments reported as part of the near-death experience – which are similar to judgements described in many religions – also support the proposition that state of mind at the time of death has a bearing on the quality of post-death existence. Those who die slow deaths have been shown to report fewer judgements, implying that they have had time to reconcile the troublesome issues in their lives. On the other hand, those who die suddenly report greater numbers of judgements after death, implying that they have died with unresolved, troubled minds.

All these insights point to the need for preparation before death. Approach it without resolving the disturbing issues that overshadow your life and you face a difficult post-death journey, a tough post-death assessment or judgement, and the prospect of an unhappy afterlife. Although this inference is clear from the near-death experience, from religious insights stretching back through the ages and from modern quantum mechanics, few people heed it; instead, they dismiss thoughts about death from their lives.

The assessment and evaluation of past behaviours is mostly ignored. Wrongs inflicted on others are brushed aside. Acts of unkindness are overlooked. Dishonest behaviours remain unacknowledged. All the anger and bitterness, the malice and spite, the rancour, greed, malevolence and animosity remains unheeded and unresolved. The physical body may die, but these issues do not die with it; instead, they face judgement and resolution once the physical phase of existence comes to a close.

All of the world's major religions – and most of the minor ones, too – have been light years ahead in recognising and reflecting the need for meaningful death preparation and the resolution of life's wrongdoings. The principle is enshrined in Catholicism, with its multiplicity of rites and pre-death proced-ures. Among them is the final confession, the last blessing and the Sacrament of Extreme Unction – or anointing – of the dying person.

This latter procedure is designed, in the words of St. James, to 'save the sick man' so that 'the Lord shall raise him up; and if he be in sins they shall be forgiven him' – clearly anticipating the judgement ahead. Nothing, however, according to Catholic doctrine, can substitute for the living of a moral and righteous life – and the acknowledgement of and atonement for sins – as proper preparation for life after death.

So important was preparation for death perceived to be that, as far back as the eighth century, Buddhism acquired its own guidebook which is best known today as *The Tibetan Book of the Dead*. In effect, the book, which is a handbook for those facing death – in other words, all of us – outlines what takes place between the point of death and the next rebirth. It is also meant to be of value to people left behind as they assist the journey of those who have passed away.

The book provides a kaleidoscope of insights to the stages of death, advising us not to be distracted or afraid, to focus on inner radiance, to recognise that we don't have a body anymore so we cannot be hurt by the bewildering apparitions we will encounter. Its references to consciousness are quite remarkable, reflecting to an extraordinary degree both the near-death experience and quantum mechanics.

Just like accounts provided by people who come back from temporary death, *The Tibetan Book of the Dead* describes the judgement facing us when we die. It outlines how a 'mirror of past actions' is held up before our eyes. All the consequences of past actions – good and bad – are presented. After being weighed, our future is then decided. Although put together 12 centuries ago, this depiction of after-death judgement might be voiced by a person returning from temporary death today.

Quite apart from the issue of independent consciousness, world religions have also been miles ahead of conventional scientists in their broader understanding and articulation of what life and the universe are about. Much of what we have read in this chapter concerning survival after death, multiple universes and how matter can never be destroyed has been preached by faiths stretching back to the earliest of times.

Jesus Christ might readily have been echoing Empedocles' theory of matter when he said, 'For dust you are and to dust you will return.' The early Egyptians might be said to have anticipated the Penrose-Hameroff view of post-death survival when they drew images of souls departing from dead bodies and travelling off to a life elsewhere. The multiple universes of

Hinduism and the views on matter and space of Buddhism would not be unfamiliar to readers of modern-day quantum physics textbooks.

Where organised religions have often lost direction – as we have seen throughout this book – is in the unfortunate inventions like Limbo, the abuse of indulgences, the exaggeration of a fiery hell, the mass of tortured theological interpretations that have distorted simple insights and beliefs, and the sheer volume of rules and regulations that have made basic doctrines opaque and incomprehensible.

Beyond that, science and religion sit comfortably alongside each other. Professor Colin Russell, former science historian at Cambridge University and the Open University, put the case well: 'The common belief that....the actual relations between religion and science over the last few centuries have been marked by deep and enduring hostility....is not only historically inaccurate, but actually a caricature so grotesque that what needs to be explained is how it could possibly have achieved any degree of respectability.'

Developing Russell's point, it is often assumed that men of science who were influential in developing major laws of matter, thermodynamics, energy and the atom were so deeply rooted in scientific methodology that they didn't believe in the existence of a God. Driven by logic and methodical reasoning, their own views of the universe are frequently assumed to have been anti-metaphysical, rejecting the existence of an afterlife or a supreme creator. Only blind, irrational belief, sceptics have argued, can allow for a God; scientific knowledge precludes that possibility.

This proposition could not be further from the truth. The German physicist who originated quantum theory, Max Planck, was deeply religious. He once remarked that although he had devoted his whole life to the study of 'the most clear headed science,' his conclusions were profoundly in favour of belief in a supreme power. 'All matter originates and exists only by virtue of a force which brings the particle of an atom to vibration and holds this most minute solar system of the atom together. We must assume behind this force the existence of a conscious and intelligent mind. This mind is the matrix of all matter,' he said.

In a comparable vein, James Joule, the English physicist whose experiments eventually culminated in the law of conservation of energy and the first law of thermodynamics, firmly believed that his work was consistent with the Bible. He wrote: 'It is manifestly absurd to suppose that the powers with which God has endowed matter can be destroyed any more than they can be created by man's agency.' The entire machinery of the universe, he concluded, 'complicated as it is, works smoothly and harmoniously....the whole being governed by the sovereign will of God.'

Numerous other scientists have held strong religious beliefs. Pascual Jordan – one of the fathers of quantum mechanics – also believed in the compatibility of science and religion, writing extensively on the matter. Ernest Walton, the Irish physicist and Nobel Prize winner, who was the first person to artificially split the atom, was a practising Methodist and advised that mankind should 'pay God the compliment of studying his work of art.' The atomic theorist, John Dalton, was a devout Quaker.

A study of Nobel Prize winners adds further support to the proposition that science and religion are compatible. Among the insights revealed in Dr. Baruch Shalev's book *100 Years of Nobel Prizes* are the following – almost three out of four Nobel Prize winners for Chemistry, from 1901–2000, identified

Christianity as their preferred faith; some two out of three Physics and Medicine winners likewise professed to be Christian. Among other religions, Judaism was strongly represented.

No matter what scientific innovation you select – Marconi's radio inventions, Babbage's first computer, Pasteur's vaccination and pasteurisation breakthroughs, Rayleigh's discovery of why the sky is blue, Damadian's first MRI scanning machine, not to mention the scientific output of Copernicus, Galileo, Newton, Faraday, Boyle and Descartes – it is clear that religion played a significant role in the personal philosophies of those involved.

Religion has also underscored the thoughts of comedian and movie-maker Woody Allen. Death has caught his attention, too, although like the rest of us he has found it easier to circumvent it as an issue for serious thought or debate. 'Death? It's ruined my life completely,' he once remarked in one of his amusing comments about the spectre that overshadows us all. He has delivered other lines, too, including 'I'm not afraid of death; I just don't want to be there when it happens' and, referring to the promise of post-death fame, 'I don't want to live on in the hearts of my countrymen; I want to live on in my apartment.'

Perhaps if Woody Allen had familiarised himself with classical physics, quantum mechanics and the near-death experience he might have had something different to say about the reality of dying. Between them, they provide a positive, compelling and comprehensive insight to our after-death survival. Collectively, they reveal that our component parts cannot perish and that our consciousness – or soul or mind, whatever you wish to call it – almost certainly survives the demise of our physical bodies. Most of all, they show that we are masters of our own afterlife – the choice of heaven or hell is ours and ours alone.

What you have read in this chapter is the closest we can get, at this point in time, to understanding what happens when the brain flatlines and the heart stops beating. All the component parts fit together. The inconsistencies that once existed disappear. Some people might be sceptical, but that is understandable. As the German philosopher Schopenhauer once remarked: 'All truth passes through three stages. First, it is ridiculed. Second, it is violently opposed. Third, it is accepted as being self-evident.'

Ultimately, the truth of after-death survival is in the telling, and this brings us back to where we began this chapter, to Elsie and her near-death experience. Hers was a remarkable journey, reflecting much of what we have learned in the pages so far and validating what modern-day science tells us about life after death. Her conclusions offer us an appealing vista ahead – a wonderful journey to a warm, loving, peaceful world, where we live on in the presence of God. Presuming that we depart with a clear conscience and an unburdened mind, the prospects are glorious, indeed.

'I believe that dying, and where we go to, will be the beginning of our life,' Elsie concludes. 'It will not be a life as we know it on earth; instead, it will be as we have always wanted it to be, as we have prepared for. All races and all creeds, all of God's family, will be there, perfect and complete. We will know each other, and we will be of the one family.

'The love that we have here on earth will be nothing compared to the love that we'll be living. Love is the ultimate and, as God's children, we will be full of it for each other. We need to love here, too. The only thing that's expected is to do your best and not wish evil to anybody....that's love, and that's what it is all about.'

ACKNOWLEDGEMENTS

There is an old saying that warns us to 'beware of the man with a single book'. An astute rule of thumb, it identifies the need to consider a broad range of viewpoints and to open our minds to a multiplicity of insights and beliefs. The conclusions of anyone who does otherwise are likely to be way off the mark.

It is a criticism that cannot be levelled at *Journey's End*. To the contrary, exhaustive research was undertaken in the course of writing this book. I have consulted many hundreds of reports, studies, manuscripts and ancient texts, as well as conducting numerous interviews. A selection of the main written sources will be credited in the pages ahead.

Few research sources can match the Egyptian Book of the Dead, Tibetan Book of the Dead, Bhagavad Gita, the Vedas and Puranas of Hinduism and, of course, the Koran, the Torah and books of the Old and New Testaments. Although written a long time ago, they contain startling insights to the process of dying. When read with open eyes – and allowing for their sometimes obscure language – they tell us almost everything we need to know about death.

Further works of great importance were compiled during the Middle Ages – that prolonged span of time stretching from the fifth to the fifteenth centuries. They range from the fifth-century *City of God* by St. Augustine to the fifteenth-century *Imitation of Christ* by Thomas à Kempis. Others include Pope Gregory I's

Dialogues, the Venerable Bede's *Ecclesiastical History of the English People*, St. Thomas Aquinas's *Summa Theologica*, and Dante's *Divine Comedy*.

Wonderful vision accounts were also produced in the latter part of the Middle Ages, including the *Treatise on St. Patrick's Purgatory* by the monk Henry of Saltrey, the *Vision of Wetti* by the monk Heito, the *Vision of Furseus* by person unknown, and the *Vision of Tundale* by the Irish itinerant monk Brother Marcus. These colourful texts were hugely popular; indeed, they were the potboilers of their time. They were also of great value to me.

Many disappointing books have been written about heaven and hell, most of them the product of fertile imaginations. That cannot be alleged about *The Book of Heaven*, edited by Carol Zaleski and Philip Zaleski, which has been useful throughout this book. Another work of wide-ranging value was *Visions of Heaven & Hell before Dante*, edited by Eileen Gardiner. Suffice to say that both texts were helpful over many chapters and I would strongly recommend them to anyone.

Regarding heaven, a number of other specific texts proved to be most useful, including *Intra Muros* by Rebecca Ruter Springer, which was published in 1898, *Four Books of Sentences* by Peter Lombard, *At the Hour of Death* by Karlis Osis and Erlendur Haraldsson, *De Contemptu Mundi* by Bernard of Cluny, and *Anecdotes de Médecine* by Pierre Jean Du Monchaux.

Other 'heavenly' source works include *Heaven* by Randy Alcorn and *The Passion of St. Perpetua, St. Felicitas, and their Companions* written by Perpetua shortly before her martyrdom in the early third century. Daisy's pre-death experience, which was recalled in the book, occurred in the mid-nineteenth century and featured in *The Journal of the American Society for Psychical Research*.

Some excellent work has been done on the issue of children and the afterlife, most notably by Dr. Elisabeth Kübler-Ross in her book *On Children and Death*, Dr. Melvin Morse in *Closer to the Light*, where he investigated childhood near-death experiences, and Sir William Barrett in his groundbreaking *Death-bed Visions*, which was published in 1926.

The issue of animals in the afterlife has been examined by many researchers and some notable books have been produced – included among them *The Dominion of Love* by Norm Phelps, *Animals and World Religions* by Lisa Kemmerer and *Vegetarian Christian Saints* by Dr. Holly H. Roberts. Do Animals Go to Heaven? by Joyce E. Salisbury, published in the *Athens Journal of Humanities & Arts* (January 2014), was also instructive.

The Other Side of Death by Jan Price, *The Truth in the Light* by Dr. Peter and Elizabeth Fenwick and *Beyond the Light* by P. M. H. Atwater also provided fascinating animal stories, as did the authors William Serdahely and Rebecca Ruter Springer. The Indian legend of Yudhisthira and his loyal dog is contained in the Sanskrit epic narrative *Mahabharata*.

The subject of hell is covered in many good books, among them *The Encyclopedia of Hell* by Miriam Van Scott and *Is Hell for Real or Does Everyone Go to Heaven?* by Timothy Keller and others. My thanks also to *Return from Tomorrow* by George Ritchie, *23 Minutes in Hell* by Bill Wiese and *A Day in Hell: Death to Life to Hope* by Nancy Botsford.

My gratitude also extends to Mark Twain's *Huckleberry Finn*; additionally to his speech before the Order of Acorns in 1901, which included his 'heaven for climate, hell for company' remark. Likewise to *Martin Luther: The Christian between God and Death* by Richard Marius, which provided me with that extraordinary excerpt about the fires of hell delivered by a medieval Italian preacher and used in the Hell chapter.

Marius's book, just mentioned, was also most helpful in the Purgatory chapter, as were *Between Saint James and Erasmus* by J. van Herwaarden and *Purgatory: Illustrated by the Lives and Legends of the Saints* by Rev. F. X. Schouppe, which was translated from French to English in 1893.

Nothing, of course, is more interesting than descriptions of, and discussions about, God and his nemesis Lucifer. Regarding the former, thanks are due once again to *Return from Tomorrow* by Dr. George Ritchie, to Arthur Yensen's *I Saw Heaven* and to *The God Delusion*, written by Richard Dawkins. Crystal McVea's comments came from an interview she did with the New York Daily News, but she has also published her experience in her book *Waking Up in Heaven*. The movie *The Ten Commandments* is likewise mentioned in the chapter and, after all these years, it is still both entertaining and instructive to watch.

Regarding that dark rogue Lucifer, *The Flowing Light of the Godhead* by Mechthild of Magdeburg (translated by Professor Frank Tobin), John Bunyan's *Visions of Heaven and Hell* and Milton's *Paradise Lost* were all indispensible. Also important were *The Generous Gambler* by poet Charles Baudelaire, *Tales, Rumors, and Gossip* by Gail de Vos and *The Devil in Fred Stonehouse: The Aesthetics of Evil After Evil* by J. Sage Elwell. For information on showband singer Joe Dolan, I am indebted to *Joe Dolan: The Official Biography* by Ronan Casey.

On the question of previous lives, or reincarnation, a number of publications proved beneficial: *The Search for Bridey Murphy* by Morey Bernstein, *I Have Lived Before: The True Story of the Reincarnation of Shanti Devi* by Sture Lönnerstrand, *Gleanings in Buddha-Fields* by the 'Irishman' Lafcadio Hearn, and an impressive investigation of a small number of case histories by Dr. Antonia Mills in her *A Replication Study: Three Cases of Children in Northern India Who are Said to Remember a Previous Life*. On the history and folklore fronts, Douglas Hyde's *A Literary History of Ireland* and W.Y. Evans-Wentz's 1911 text *The Fairy-Faith in Celtic Countries* were also of use.

What You Take to Heaven by Michael Harold Brown was most valuable in The Book of Life chapter, as was E. A. Wallis Budge's *The Egyptian Heaven and Hell* and his translation of the ancient papyrus of Ani. St. Boniface's story quoted in the chapter is contained in one of his many letters, with the particular one used in the book dating from 716/717.

Quantum mechanics is a fascinating, although complex, area of study. The four main quantum theories focused on in *Journey's End* are featured in the following papers or publications: *Brain, Mind, and the Structure of Reality* by Prof. Paul L. Nunez; *Consciousness and the Universe* by Prof. Roger Penrose, Stuart Hameroff and many others; *The Theory of the Universal Wave Function*, which is the Princeton PhD thesis of Hugh Everett III; and *Biocentrism: How Life and Consciousness are the Keys to Understanding the True Nature of the Universe* by Robert Lanza. My thanks also to Dr. Baruch Shalev's book *100 Years of Nobel Prizes*.

The double-slit experiment, which first came to life when performed by Thomas Young in 1801, has been replicated time and again and is referred to or featured in virtually every quantum mechanics textbook produced in modern times. Other worthwhile books include *What Happens after Death? An Unbiased Examination of Various Popular Theories* by Nicolas E. Wright; *God and the Multiverse: Humanity's Expanding View of the Cosmos* by Victor J. Stenger; *Physics of the Soul: The Quantum Book of Living, Dying, Reincarnation, and Immortality* by Amit Goswami; *Quantum: A Guide for the Perplexed* by Jim Al-Khalili; and *The Many Worlds of Hugh Everett III* by Peter Byrne.

This book was conceptualised and written in both counties Waterford and Cork, where so many people were helpful and supportive. I would particularly like to single out a wonderful dog named Frankie who took me for numerous long walks, and an equally wonderful horse named Princess whose zest for living and affectionate nature kept me going through difficult times. They were both vital to me in writing this book.

My admiration also to the numerous medical professionals whose expertise literally kept me alive. Barbara Ryan and Linda Monahan, both of Typeform, made invaluable contributions to text layout and to cover design, while the company's production director Roy Thewlis was also most helpful. In addition, without the numerous near-death experience accounts this project would never have been initiated never mind completed. My gratitude goes out to all those who told me their stories.

Finally, I am indebted to my wife Úna O'Hagan, who advised me at all stages throughout the research and writing of *Journey's End*. This was no easy book to put together, with the work stretching over a long period of time. She was always there for me, encouraging me, advising me and involving herself in all aspects of the book's production. If ever a big 'thank you' is due to anyone, it is due to her.

GOING HOME

IRISH STORIES FROM THE EDGE OF DEATH

Colm Keane

Going Home contains the most comprehensive insights ever provided by Irish people into what happens when we die.

Many of those interviewed have clinically died – some after heart attacks, others after long illnesses or accidents. They have returned to claim – 'There is life after death!'

Most have travelled through dark tunnels and entered intensely bright lights. Some have been greeted by dead relatives and met a superior being. All have floated outside their bodies and watched themselves down below.

Those left behind describe visions of relatives who passed away. The book also acquaints us with the latest scientific research.

Award-winning journalist Colm Keane has spoken to people from all corners of Ireland and recounts their stories.

Based on years of research, Going Home provides us with the most riveting insight we may ever get into where we go after death.

Reviews of Going Home

'Fascinating' *Irish Daily Mail*
'Intriguing' *Sunday World*
'A beautiful, satisfying, comforting book' *Radio Kerry*

THE DISTANT SHORE

MORE IRISH STORIES FROM THE EDGE OF DEATH

Colm Keane

The Distant Shore is packed with a wealth of new Irish stories about life after death.

Extraordinary accounts of what takes place when we die are featured throughout. Reunions with deceased relatives and friends, and encounters with a 'superior being', are included.

Visions of dead family members are vividly described. The book also examines astonishing premonitions of future events.

This compilation was inspired by the huge response to Colm Keane's number one bestseller Going Home – a groundbreaking book that remained a top seller for six months.

Containing new material and insights, The Distant Shore is indispensable reading for those who want to know what happens when we pass away.

Reviews of *The Distant Shore*

'Amazing new stories' *Irish Independent*

'Terrific, wonderful read' *Cork 103 FM*

'A source of genuine comfort to anyone who has suffered a bereavement' *Western People*

FOREWARNED

EXTRAORDINARY IRISH STORIES OF PREMONITIONS AND DREAMS

Colm Keane

Did you ever have a feeling that something bad was going to happen? Perhaps you dreamt of a future event? Maybe you had a 'gut feeling' that an illness, death, car crash or some other incident was about to occur?

Most Irish people, at various stages of their lives, have experienced a forewarning of the future. It may reveal itself as a sense of unease. Alternatively, it may be more intense and involve a terrifying foreboding. Perhaps it brings good news.

Forewarned is the first Irish enquiry into this intriguing phenomenon. Crammed with fascinating stories, the book also presents the latest scientific evidence proving that the future is closer to our minds than we think.

Reviews of *Forewarned*

'Amazing stories' *Belfast Telegraph*

'Authenticity of experience is written all over these reports' *The Irish Catholic*

'A fascinating read' *Soul & Spirit*

HEADING FOR THE LIGHT

THE 10 THINGS THAT HAPPEN WHEN YOU DIE

Colm Keane

This explosive book reveals the truth about what happens when we die.

The ten stages we go through when we die are outlined for the very first time. They establish conclusively that death is a warm, happy experience and is nothing to fear.

Based on five years of research, the author has drawn from the real-life stories of people who have temporarily died and returned to life.

This definitive book provides you with all you need to know about the stages of death as we head for the light.

Reviews of *Heading for the Light*

'Absolutely fascinating' *RTÉ One*
'Provides much pause for thought' *Sunday Independent*
'The mysteries of dying and death from those who know'
The Irish Catholic

Capel Island Press
Baile na nGall, Ring, Dungarvan,
County Waterford, Ireland
Email: capelislandpress@hotmail.com